Comparing National Approaches to Maritime Security in the Post-9/11 Era

Peter C. Avis

Centre for Foreign Policy Studies

Library and Archives Canada Cataloguing in Publication

Avis, Peter C. (Peter Charles), 1957-

Comparing national approaches to maritime security in the post-9/11
era / by Peter C. Avis.

(Maritime security occasional paper ; no. 14)
Includes bibliographical references.
ISBN 1-896440-47-9

 1. Sea-power—Canada. 2. Canada—Military policy. 3. Military
policy—Case studies. 4. National security—Canada. 5. National
security—Case studies. 6. Canada—Defenses. I. Dalhousie
University. Centre for Foreign Policy Studies II. Title. III. Series.

VA400.A94 2005   359'.03'0971   C2004-907290-0

TABLE OF CONTENTS

LIST OF TABLES

ACKNOWLEDGEMENTS

This has been a wonderful way to spend one's 47th year. I have learned a great deal and I feel that I have played a small part in advancing the study of maritime security in Canada. I would like to thank Dr. Martin Rudner, my supervisor, for his sage counsel and steady hand on the helm during the initial stages of writing the paper. I would also like to thank Dr. David Carment, my advisor, for his enthusiasm for teaching and his dedication to finding better ways to invoke strategic early warning. I wish to thank the Department of National Defence, the navy and, in particular, Vice-Admiral Ron Buck for allowing me to take this precious time for widening my horizons. I would be remiss if I did not thank Vivian Cummins, Cindy Halden and Brenda Sutherland of the Norman Paterson School of International Affairs for cheerfully directing me down the correct administrative paths throughout the process. Finally, Dr. Ann Griffiths of Dalhousie University was a great help in the final hours of the editing process prior to publication.

CHAPTER 1
THE SEA MATTERS

Introduction

The advent of global-level terrorism, most vividly portrayed by the events of 11 September 2001, has altered the global security landscape in such a way as to necessitate significant changes in the way governments approach security. Due to the amorphous, unpredictable and asymmetric nature of terrorism,[1] countries that feel particularly threatened have re-written existing or initiated new national security strategies to cope with threats that are not adequately dealt with in outdated Cold War-oriented policies. National security, of course, spans the whole collectivity of security concerns—foreign influence, perimeter and border issues, internal concerns, as well as all flows of humanity, goods and information that interconnect the external and the internal concerns of states through aerospatial, maritime, terrestrial, or cybernetic means.

Modern terrorist organizations, such as Al Qaida, plot to thwart national security strategies by exploiting the seams and the vulnerabilities in this complex environment of state-focused security.[2] Their disconnected and independent existence apart from the international system of sovereign states makes them all the more elusive and dangerous for their targets—the interconnected nation-states of the international, globalizing system.

A full study of national security would necessarily have to examine such diverse areas of government endeavour as politics, economics, transportation (air, land and sea), health, communications, law enforcement, intelligence, critical infrastructure protection, and so on. This sort of larger strategic landscape exists for all countries and links into both domestic and international concerns. The potential breadth and complexity of such a study would make it daunting to undertake. A more feasible approach would be to identify the key areas of national security and examine them separately. This must be done, however, with the overarching understanding that the elements of national security are interlinked and must eventually be married together for optimum value.

National Security

National security is a state that is achieved through government actions that deal with "threats that have the potential to undermine security of the state or society."[3] It "represents the preservation of the nation's people, resources, and culture."[4] The conceptual sphere of national security rests between and is strongly linked to the spheres of personal security and international security. Thus, a criminal offence that may threaten personal security but does not threaten the security of the state would not be considered a national security issue. Similarly, there can be threats to portions of the international system that do not have an impact on a particular state's security. However, the areas of overlap between the national security sphere and the other two spheres contain numerous examples of threats that have the capacity to seriously impair the security of the state. When one investigates the overlap between national security and international security, issues that reside there such as terrorism, illegal immigration, disease transmission, environmental disasters, cyber-crime and transnational organized crime shine forth as serious threats.

States vary in their capabilities and resources, but all states must be able to provide security for themselves. According to

Alex Tewes, L. Rayner and K. Kavanaugh, "National power is translated into national security when it addresses successfully the challenges facing the country across the various security sectors."[5] The subsets or sectors of national security that deal with these issues are aviation security, maritime security, border security and cyber-security. This monograph concerns itself with maritime security as a subset of national security.

Maritime Security

Maritime security is, thus, a subset of national security. It is a state's ability to address the security challenges that reside in its maritime environment. A state cannot be secure without possessing the ability to protect its maritime interests, its coasts and its maritime approaches. Maritime security has components in all levels of security—personal, national and international.[6] However, for the purposes of this monograph, it is the security overlap between the national and international spheres in which a state deals with both internal and external issues that affect national security that will be discussed. Thus, the focus will be on how states approach the security of their shipping, their ports, their internal and territorial waters, their offshore facilities, international waters, and national interests in foreign ports. The terms "maritime security" and "marine security" are both used throughout the resource material dealing with this subject. The use of "marine security" is most prevalent in documentation that emanates from the transportation sector of numerous governments. For this study the two terms will be said to have the same meaning and, as "maritime security" is preferred by the author, it will be the term that is utilized.

In today's world there are many different concerns and potential threats to a state's security so why does maritime security matter? Why is it necessary? What is happening on the oceans and in the ports of the world that would make one stand up and take notice? Many people are unaware of the magnitude and importance of activity that takes place on the world's oceans and in its ports. Over 50% of the world's population lives within 80 kilometres of the sea and that percentage is estimated to rise to 75% in 25 years.[7] There are approximately 93,000 merchant ships being received at the world's 8,200 ports and these ships are transporting over 5.7 billion tons of cargo annually.[8] Due to the efficiencies of containerized shipping in an inter-modal global transportation system, 99% of the volume and 85% of the value of all intercontinental trade flows across the seas.[9] As the Navy League of Canada phrased it, "The oceans are the great highways upon which much of the world's business depends and the sea remains a key means of communication between states as well as between communities."[10]

While trade and communication are very important, other key maritime interests include exploitation of natural resources, passenger transport, scientific research and recreation. Combined, these interests can account for a significant portion of the economies of many states—in fact, many states are dependent on the maritime dimension of their economy for their national well-being. The global economy furnishes numerous examples. The trade of bulk commodities (coal, iron ore, grain, crude oil) between producers and consumer countries, which are generally located thousands of miles from each other, depends strongly on shipping. Without shipping, the demand would be impossible to meet. The Middle East is by far the largest producer of crude oil in the world; its product is primarily transported by sea to Europe, North America and Japan. To fuel its powerful economy, Japan imports 90 per cent of its energy—all of which arrives in tankers. The United States and Germany are also dependent to a lesser extent on energy resources that arrive by sea.[11] From a different angle, Norway and the United Kingdom, with their North Sea oil exploitation, are net energy producers. In Norway's case, this source of wealth has allowed it the flexibility it needed to remain separate from the European Union—an important national decision.[12] Suffice to say that maritime economic activities are crucial for the livelihood of many states.

Canada is a country whose economy is dependent on trade— the total value of trade has recently been in the range of $740-760 billion (Canadian dollars (CAD)). Out of that total, approximately $100 billion (CAD) derives from international maritime trade— or 14 per cent of overall trade.[13] Canada's unique place as neighbour to the world's superpower sees 80 per cent of total trade taking place with the United States. Twenty per cent of this Canada-US trade takes place on the water. Over 350 million tonnes of cargo are moved through Canadian ports each year, two-thirds of which comes from international trade—this ratio represents the sustained flow of refined products and raw materials in and out of Canada.[14]

It must be noted that 60 per cent of incoming cargo containers that are handled in Canadian ports are destined for the United States, a situation that requires Canada to maintain American confidence in return for sustained business.[15] Canada's marine sector employs over 30,000 people who generate average annual revenues of $2.6 billion (CAD). Cruise ship passengers contributed a further $1 billion (CAD) to the economy.[16] Furthermore, as a net exporter of energy, Canada has a growing offshore oil and gas industry which currently exports 5 billion barrels.[17] Add to these statistics fisheries, research, recreation, international ferry revenues, plus the potential of the Arctic, and one sees a thriving industry sector that is important to Canadians. Thus, many Canadians depend on some aspect of the ocean for their livelihoods. It is ironic that despite the apparent indifference of Canadians to the country's maritime dimensions, they are widely dependent on it.

Vulnerabilities in the Maritime Security Environment
Even though maritime activity is so important to the global

economy, and in turn to certain national economies, it is vulnerable to modern threats, whether they are criminal, terrorist, or otherwise. This vulnerability is not surprising when one considers how open trade via the oceans has become over the last 20 years. Due to the dramatic success of container shipping which fuels the efficiency of the global inter-modal transportation system, governments and private corporations have concentrated on economic progress and freedom of navigation to enhance intercontinental trade flows. The advent of "hub-and-spoke networks" in the container industry combined with "just-in-time" supply chains has led to the increased strategic importance of hub-ports and geographic choke-points.[18] These key points of convergence are few in number and account for an increasingly constricted sea-borne trade flow. The implication of this constriction is decreased flexibility or potential breakdown in the event of natural or man-made disturbance. As Daniel Coulter has noted "The importance of energy and container traffic essentially means that the "hub" container and bulk commodity ports as well as other choke-points now form the vulnerable "underbelly" of the global economy."[19] It is clear that unless these strategic points are well managed and protected, they represent important vulnerabilities to the global economy.

Individual states have also discovered vulnerability gaps throughout their maritime systems. While there is much effort being focused on filling international and national gaps since the attacks of 9/11, this process has only just begun and will take years to implement. In general, states have not made themselves aware of the global traffic flow and struggle to track individual vessels as they approach their home coastlines. The ability of most states to form a complete picture of the totality of maritime traffic either globally or even in their own sovereign waters, unlike the clarity of the air traffic picture, is inadequate.

The capability of government departments to share information and collaborate with other departments, civilian agencies and the maritime organizations of other countries has been found wanting. The Cold War propensity to maintain "a tightly compartmented flow of information" in "organizational stove-pipes" has hampered national ability to integrate intelligence and information sharing efforts—particularly between law enforcement groups and intelligence agencies.[20] Due to the focus on economic progress, physical security of ports, ships, offshore facilities and other maritime interests has been given a low priority. A mishap in one port could cause a chain reaction that would magnify vulnerability. As US authorities point out,

> consider the fact that an attack that shut down a major American port for even a few days could devastate the regional economy it serves ... if we had to shut down all our ports and check all of the ships for terrorists—commercial shipping would be shut down for months.[21]

Furthermore, the Defence Science Advisory Board of Canada found in its report *The Asymmetric Threat* that, should a terrorist group attain weapons of mass destruction (nuclear, biological, or chemical), "the maritime environment poses the likeliest venue for bringing such devices to or close to North America" due to the minimal inspection rates of containers entering North American ports.[22] Finally, the ability to respond to a maritime threat, not just the resources to physically defend, but the ability to engage a timely and coordinated display of national will, is often beyond the means of many countries.

A Study Within Maritime Security: Methodology

We have now examined the new maritime battlespace and the importance and vulnerability of maritime security within it. The following series of questions form the basis for the rest of this monograph. How do Australia, Norway and the Netherlands (all

Western-style democracies which have an indirect relationship to terrorism) prioritize their approaches to maritime security? What are the best practices stemming from a comparison of these cases? How can these best practices help to improve the approach to maritime security of other states, particularly those of Canada?

It would appear that countries which perceive a direct threat to their homeland are likely to weigh their priorities in favour of cooperative and proactive approaches in their approaches to national and maritime security. By enacting preventive approaches, these countries actively seek to prevent major attacks on their native soil and to neutralize the threat before it takes shape far beyond their borders.

To prove this hypothesis, this monograph will use case study analysis. Existing documentation in Canada, while showing an awareness of the possibility of using preventive methods, tends to focus on crisis management and consequence management in order to obtain the desired level of national security from terrorist threats. To respond to the research questions, this monograph will examine three countries that differ from Canada in many ways yet have certain strong similarities to Canada and all are in the process of prioritizing their approaches concerning national security. They have each chosen different paths to increase their maritime security based on their individual national situations. Furthermore, they are implementing policy at a rapid pace to increase their government's capability to challenge the threat of terrorism.

The choice of these countries was based on particular criteria that would lead the ensuing research towards useful discoveries about maritime security for Canada. The first and most important criterion in the choice of these countries was that they are *not* the United States. While there are significant lessons to be learned from our superpower neighbour, the American republican system of government is fundamentally different from Canada's parliamentary system that is based on the Westminster model. The two forms of polity are dissimilar and difficult to compare. Moreover, the United States has the largest economy in the world with a per capita Gross Domestic Product (GDP) of $37,800 in 2003.[23] Canada is a middle power, with a tenth of the population of the United States, a much more modest economy, and a per capita GDP of $29,700. Thus, the US capacity to change homeland security systems is somewhat overwhelming in comparison. Finally, the United States suffered a catastrophic attack by terrorists on its home territory—a fact that dramatically altered the American psyche with respect to homeland security. The effect of the 9/11 attacks was much less severe for Canadians. The attacks were seen to be significant and dangerous but not necessarily aimed at Canada in particular.

Australia, the Netherlands and Norway, like the United States and Canada are democratic states that have strong links to the sea. All are interlinked at certain levels in the uniquely intimate Anglo-American intelligence cooperation under the UK-USA Agreement: Canada and Australia as "Second Parties" and Norway and the Netherlands as more limited "Third Parties."[24] Unlike the United States, however, Australia, the Netherlands, Norway and Canada have the economic capacity of middle powers. As noted, Canada's per capita GDP was $29,700 in 2003, and the other three had the following figures for 2003:

- Australia, $28,900;
- the Netherlands, $28,600; and
- Norway (which has increased strongly in recent years), $37,700.[25]

These healthy figures have a strong relationship to trade in all four countries. All four have a trade surplus which is a key strength in their economies. The export of natural resources is a mainstay for Canada, Norway and Australia, while the Netherlands concentrates on its strength as a European transportation hub to export industrially processed goods such as food processing, chemicals, refined fuels and electrical machinery.[26]

As noted, Canada is a trade-dependent country and has a strong maritime trade sector. Norway "is highly dependent on its oil production and international oil prices; in 1999, oil and gas accounted for 35% of exports."[27] With the largest merchant marine fleet (714 ships) of the three case-countries, Norway is "a major shipping nation, with a high dependence on international trade."[28] Furthermore, Norway has a rare external debt of zero and has used its maritime-based oil revenues to save over $110 billion (USD) in a government fund for future contingencies.[29] Although it does not have a huge coast line, the Netherlands derives more than two-thirds of GDP from merchandise and service trade,[30] and depends on its large merchant fleet (635 ships) and the hub-port of Rotterdam, the world's largest port, to bolster its open economy. Finally, Australia is benefiting from a series of economic reforms which aim for competitive status as a producer and exporter of traditional resources as well as recent additions of manufactured goods and technology. Indeed, it "transformed itself from an inward looking, import-substitution country to an internationally competitive, export-oriented one."[31] An island continent, it has a very small merchant navy (51 ships); however, its modest population (19.8 million) matched with wealth in natural resources attracts international shipping to engage in $180 billion (USD) of maritime trade in mining and agricultural goods which account for 57% of Australia's goods and services exports.[32] Table 1 below summarizes pertinent national data from a maritime perspective. Clearly, if a major attack on the maritime systems of any of these countries took place, the economic repercussions would be severe. Therefore, it is probable that they would all be sensitive to security threats in the maritime sector and would develop policies to protect what economic strengths they possess.

It is also important to consider national immigration policies. Since planned immigration was initiated in Australia in the 1960s, the population has risen from seven million to almost 20 million. Recently, however, immigration policy has become increasingly selective—the target is between 100,000 and 110,000 migrants annually. Currently, approximately 20% of the total population of Australia is non-Western/European.[33] The Netherlands, which has long been known to welcome immigrants and refugees, has a tradition in European institutions for free movement of people and goods across common borders. Currently, 10% of the population has a non-Western background, the major contributors being Morocco, Dutch Antilles, Surinam and Turkey.[34] Norway has an immigrant population that makes up 7.3% of the overall population, 70% of whom are non-Western.[35]

In all these countries, including Canada, the majority of the immigrant population lives in major urban centres, they experience the most unemployment, they often feel non-integrated, and for the most part have lower incomes than the rest of the population. This division creates tension between immigrants and citizens. The strain on the immigration societies that this situation

Table 1: Comparison of Countries

Country	Per Capita GDP (000)	Population (in millions)	Coast Line (kms)	Major Ports	Focus of Trade	Merchant Marine (# ships)	Relative Maritime Importance Indicators
Australia	$28.9	20	25,760	Brisbane Freemantle Melbourne	export of natural resources	51	57% goods and services exports go by sea
Netherlands	$28.6	16.3	415	Rotterdam Amsterdam	transport hub for Europe	635	world's largest container hub-port
Norway	$37.7	4.5	21,900	Oslo Stavanger Bergen	export of natural resources	714	oil and gas exports account for 35% of exports
Canada	$29.7	32.5	202,800	Vancouver Montreal Halifax	export of natural resources	119	14% of overall export trade goes by sea

creates is a sensitive area for the governments involved. While all these countries want to maintain immigration, there is a growing unease about security in society.[36] In particular, since 9/11 and the terrorist bombings in Bali and Madrid, immigrants with Muslim affiliations have experienced criticism and scrutiny. A report from the General Intelligence and Investigation Agency (AIVD), the Dutch secret service, stated that "there are approximately 150 persons in Holland who have contacts with the Al-Qaeda terrorist organization."[37]

Each of the subject countries has come to the revelation that the issue of security is not only a challenge from the outside of the borders, but an internal problem as well. Thus, in their struggle to maintain national security and the traditional openness to immigration, each of them will have to confront the modern problem of a multi-directional threat—a task that challenges the way that traditional government organizational structure has been constructed. The fact that all of the subject countries have major ports (Rotterdam/Amsterdam, Oslo, Brisbane/Freemantle/Melbourne, and Montreal/Vancouver) that are also major urban centres where immigrants cluster situates maritime security concerns at the forefront of government agendas.

This monograph will draw out key government activities that illuminate how each case-country prioritizes its approach to maritime security. It will prioritize the key factors using a number of conditional antecedents to test predictions.[38] These conditional antecedents are:

- resource allocation;
- machinery of government;
- national legislation;
- policy development;
- information sharing,
- intelligence collection; and
- assessment and warning organizations.

Government responses can be categorized in order to illustrate shared duties, overlap of cultures and clarity of purpose.

A national maritime security system is composed of a number of essential activities that can be grouped into four general categories.[39] These four categories are:

- domain awareness;
- safeguarding;
- responsiveness; and
- collaboration.

Domain awareness is the activity which enables a state to be aware of and comprehend what is happening and who is present in all areas of maritime responsibility. It is made up of surveillance and intelligence efforts to build a comprehensive picture of a state's maritime zones and interest areas—both domestic and international. Domain awareness seeks clarity through liaison and coordination between national and international security, intelligence and law enforcement groups to integrate, develop and disseminate critical data related to maritime security. Successful domain awareness leads to national alertness in the right areas at the right time on a continual basis. In this way, government decision-makers are better able to manage risk and take appropriate action before, during and after a threatening event.

Safeguarding is the activity that ensures the physical security of maritime infrastructure such as ports and vessels as well as other critical infrastructure in or around areas of maritime responsibility (including offshore platforms). It also enhances security of personnel by creating an environment which precludes terrorist or criminal activity and prevents potentially threatening persons or devices from entering a country or any part of its maritime system.

Responsiveness is the activity that executes the national will to enforce the law or to take military action to prevent imminent threats and to apprehend perpetrators. It includes all enforcement efforts of all relevant police forces, mandated security agencies and military units, both foreign and domestic, to intercept and capture terrorists, criminals, or other threats to national security.

Collaboration is central to successful maritime security policy, especially given the changed battlespace with its informational and ephemeral qualities as described above. Collaboration is different from the other three activities in that it can be seen as an "enabler" activity for all parts of maritime security. It includes the ideas of information sharing, coordination, cooperation and unified action for resolution of security problems. As such, collaboration tends to be preventive in nature. It entails horizontal sharing of information among government departments, intelligence agencies and law enforcement groups as well as vertical sharing between first responders, regional agencies, federal agencies and international agencies. It is viewed as a critical piece of the national and maritime security system in that shared knowledge and information are integral cornerstones to prevention and successful prosecution. Collaboration is important in the development of national risk management strategies.

These four activities can be superimposed across all the geographic zones of a state's maritime security responsibility. Governments use the assets they possess in security-oriented departments to carry out these four activities in aid of maritime security. The activities can apply to ships, home ports, foreign ports, offshore platforms, internal waters, international waters and every part of the maritime environment that belongs or is related to a country. This includes inter-modal connections and cyber linkages as well. After one superimposes the activities across the various zones, it is evident that security requirements are increasingly information-based the farther one is from one's own country. The requirements tend to become more physical and response-oriented as one draws near home.[40] Collaboration and domain awareness are proactive and preventive in nature, whereas safeguarding and responsiveness tend to be more reactive.

This monograph will produce a list of security approaches by examining these four essential activities in each of the case-countries. And through comparative observations across the cases, a list of best practices will be created. In *Benchmarking for Best Practices in the Public Sector*, the authors define and address the criteria for "best practices" in government and the public sector. According to this study, a "best practice" can be defined broadly as "anything better than your current practice."[41] While this general definition has some merit in that it highlights the relativity to the user's needs, the authors point out that it is too broad to be useful in selecting the top performing approaches among a group of approaches. A best practice blends together the ideas of mission success and steady improvement of procedures and practices over time.

Therefore, a best practice is not just a good idea, but an idea that has been proven in practice for a period that is worthy of assessment. (For government activities such a period would be at least one to two years given that audit functions often move in synch with yearly budget cycles. For activities that are undertaken by private business, the period can be much shorter.) A best practice must have tangible results or at least a "recognized positive outcome" that can be observed through awards, media attention, or other positive indicators.[42] Thus, it would have a direct impact on the problem at hand. It must be noted that in this study a best practice might in some cases be a practice that *prevents* an event from happening—and it is extremely difficult to assess the efficacy of a policy that is intended to prevent an event. It is hard to tell if indeed the activity prevented the event or if the event did not occur for some other unrelated reason. However, the practice may have a positive impact on some more commonplace activities that are related to the security event (illegal immigration, for instance). A positive outcome in this sort of related event would give an acceptable indication of a similar positive security outcome. And finally, a best practice must have local importance to the organization that is searching for improvement. The approach does not have to be identical for every importing organization, but a best practice should be adaptable elsewhere.[43]

For the purposes of this study, best practices are defined as processes or approaches which (a) are successful over time, (b) display a recognized positive outcome, and (c) have local importance to Canada. To be a best practice, an approach must fulfill the requirements of *all three* criteria.

Observation of these best practices will offer an idea of the relationship between the perception of threat in a given country and the maritime security approaches it selects to cope with the challenge. The usefulness of best practices to other countries will perhaps present areas for improvement for Canada.

Conclusion

The sea matters to Canada and the case-countries selected for this study. Maritime activities are extremely important to the national well-being of all four states. And yet, despite the importance of the sea, maritime shipping and related infrastructure are vulnerable to attacks and in the post-9/11 world terrorism has been linked to maritime security.

Governments respond to threats by organizing to protect themselves and their national interests. Comparing the approaches to maritime security of three states that have important similarities to Canada may create synergy in policy development and allow us to learn from the best practices of other like countries.

Notes

1.   Department of National Defence, *Strategic Assessment 2002*

(Ottawa: Directorate of Strategic Analysis Policy Planning Division Policy Group, 2002), pp. 11,110.

2. Bruce Berkowitz, "Intelligence and the War on Terrorism," in *Orbis: A Journal of World Affairs*, Vol. 46, No. 2 (Spring 2002), p. 292.

3. Canada, Privy Council Office, *Securing an Open Society: Canada's National Security Policy* (Ottawa: Privy Council Office, 2004), p. 3.

4. Vice-Admiral (Ret'd) Gary Garnett, Navy League of Canada. Opening statement for his interview with The Standing Senate Committee on National Security and Defence, Ottawa, 12 May 2003.

5. Alex Tewes, L. Rayner, and K. Kavanaugh, *A Foundation Paper on Australia's Maritime Strategy* (Canberra: Australian Government Publishing Service, 2002), pp. 16-17. A research paper prepared at client request and made available to the Joint Standing Committee on Foreign Affairs, Defence, and Trade.

6. Canada, Privy Council Office, *Securing an Open Society: Canada's National Security Policy*),p. 4.

7.   Reuven Leopold, "The Next Naval Revolution," in *Jane's Navy International* (January/February 1996), p. 12.

8. Canada, Department of National Defence, Directorate of Maritime Strategy, "Maritime Future Security Environment 2004-2025," in Friends of the Navy Presentations (Ottawa: National Defence Headquarters, 2004).

9. Navy Element: Command and General Staff College, "Command of the Seas" (2 June, 2004). Available from http://www-cgsc.army.mil/navelm/quotes/command.asp (Cited 15 September 2004).

10. Navy League of Canada, "Canada, An Incomplete Maritime Nation," in *Maritime Affairs* (Ottawa: The Navy League of Canada, 2003), p. 4.

11. Benjamin Barber, *Jihad vs. McWorld* (New York: Ballantine Books, 2001), p. 42.

12. *Ibid.*

13. Canada, Department of Transport, *Enhancing the Security of Cana-*

da's *Marine Transportation System* (Ottawa: Interdepartmental Marine Security Working Group, 2004), p. 3.

14. Navy League of Canada, "Canada, An Incomplete Maritime Nation," p. 6.

15. Canada, Department of Transport, The *Canadian Marine Act – Beyond Tomorrow: Report of the Review Panel to the Minister of Transport* (Ottawa: Transport Canada, 2003), p. 9. Available from http://www.tc.gc.ca/pol/en/Report/tp1407b/tp1407b.htm (Cited 15 September 2004).

16. Canada, Department of Transport, *Enhancing the Security of Canada's Marine Transportation System,* p. 3.

17. Navy League of Canada, "Canada, An Incomplete Maritime Nation," p. 6.

18. Daniel Coulter, "Globalization of Maritime Commerce: The Rise of Hub Ports," in Sam J. Tangredi (ed.), *Globalization and Maritime Power* (Washington: National Defense University, 2002), p. 134. Available from http://www.ndu.edu/inss/books/Books_2002/Globalization_and_Maritime_Power_Dec_02/ 08_ch07.htm (Cited 15 September 2004).

19. Peter Haydon, "Sea Power and Maritime Strategy in the 21st Century: A "Medium" Power Perspective," in *Maritime Security Occasional Paper No. 10* (Halifax: The Centre for Foreign Policy Studies, 2000), p. 15.

20. Bruce Berkowitz, "Spying in the Post-September 11 World," in *Hoover Digest* 20 (Fall 2003), p. 5. Available from http://www-hoover.stanford.edu/publications/digest/034/berkowitz.html (Cited 15 September 2004).

21. Jenn Stewart, "Agencies Detail Plans for Seaport Security," in *Scripps Howard Foundation Wire* (January 2004). Quotation taken from an interview with Senator Jon Kyl, Chairman of the Senate Judiciary Subcommittee on Terrorism. Available from http://www.axcessnews.com/national_012804a.shtml (Cited 15 September 2004).

22. Canada, Department of National Defence, Defence Science Advisory Board, *DSAB Report 01/13 on The Asymmetric Threat* (Ottawa: DSAB, May 2002), p. 26.

23. "United States," *The World Factbook 2004*, updated 11 May 2004.

Available from http://www.cia.gov/cia/publications/factbook/geos/us.html (Cited 15 September 2004).

24. Martin Rudner, "Hunters and Gatherers: The Intelligence Coalition Against Islamic Terrorism," in *International Journal of Intelligence and CounterIntelligence*, Vol. 17, No. 2 (Summer 2004), p. 197.

25. *The World Factbook 2004.* The Purchasing Power Parity (PPP) method used in the CIA Factbook for calculating per capita GDP involves the use of standardized international dollar weights, which are applied to the quantities of final goods and services produced in a given economy. The PPP method is quite reliable for estimating and comparing the economic strength and well-being of OECD countries.

26. *Ibid.*

27. *Ibid.*

28. "Norway," *Geography and Map of Norway*, About.com website. Available from http://geography.about.com/library/cia/blcnorway.htm (Cited 15 September 2004).

29. "Norway Background Notes," The US Department of State website. Available from http://www.state.gov/r/pa/ei/bgn/3421.htm (Cited 15 September 2004).

30. "Netherlands Background Notes," US Department of State website. Available from http://www.state.gov/r/pa/ei/bgn/3204pf.htm (Cited 15 September 2004).

31. "Australia Background Notes," US Department of State website. Available from http://www.state.gov/r/pa/ei/bgn/2698.htm (Cited 15 September 2004).

32. *Ibid.*

33. Australia, Department of Immigration and Multicultural and Indigenous Affairs, "Australian Immigration Fact Sheet: Over Fifty Years of Post-War Migration," The Australian Department of Immigration website. Available from http://www.immi.gov.au/facts/04fifty.htm (Cited 15 September 2004).

34. "Statistics Netherlands: Population," in Statistics Netherlands website. Available from http://statline.cbs.nl/StatWeb/Start.asp?lp=Search/Search&LA=EN&DM=SLEN (Cited 15 September 2004).

35. "Statistics Norway: Immigration and Immigrants 2003," in Statistics Norway website. Available from http://www.ssb.no/english/subjects/02/sa_innvand_en/main.html (Cited 15 September 2004).

36. *Ibid.*

37. "Secret Service Warns of Terrorist Attacks," *Dutch News Digest* (29 April 2004). Available from http://www.dnd.nl/showarticle.php3?newsID=14726 (Cited 15 September 2004).

38. The conditional antecedents are common factors that apply to each of the countries and that allow the study to filter the important government actions out of the mix and identify key activities that are relevant to this study.

39. Canada, Department of Transport, *Enhancing the Security of Canada's Marine Transportation System*, p. 3.

40. Captain (N) Peter Avis, "Surveillance and Canadian Maritime Domestic Security," *Canadian Military Journal*, Vol. 4, No. 1 (Spring 2003), p. 11.

41. Patricia Keehley, et al., *Benchmarking for Best Practices in the Public Sector: Achieving Performance Breakthroughs in Federal, State, and Local Agencies* (San Francisco: Jossey-Bass Publishers, 1997), p. 19.

42. *Ibid.*, p. 26.

43. *Ibid.*, p. 24.

CHAPTER 2
THE NEW THREAT AND
GOVERNMENT RESPONSE

The Threat to Maritime Security

In the complex and intertwined global system that exists today, it is clear that national well-being depends greatly on interaction between states. Much of that interaction is related to trade. An important amount of that trade-oriented activity takes place in the maritime environment—in ships and in ports. Furthermore, the trade that moves in ships and through ports is connected to other environments and other modes of the supply chain that fuel the interconnected economies of the participating states. Therefore, it is important for states to maintain and improve their ability to interact in the world marketplace. This includes their ability to use the oceans and their tributary waters.

In the absence of any direct threat, an important sector of a state's economy that has known vulnerabilities would do little to inspire heavy investment in protection and security. But there are *real and serious* threats to the global maritime sector. The Royal Navy's First Sea Lord and Chief of the Naval Staff has noted that there is solid intelligence to show that Al Qaida has plans to target merchant shipping in an effort to disrupt world trade. According to Admiral Sir Alan West, "What we've noticed is that Al Qaida and other organizations have an awareness about maritime trade … they've realized how important it is for world trade in general … we are aware that they have plans and (that) they've looked at this."[1] There are threats to shipping and maritime infrastructure as well as threats to national security that could arrive via maritime means. Even without a terrorist threat, maritime means have been used to advance criminal activities that threaten Western well-being—for example, it has been possible for criminal organizations to smuggle drugs and people via merchant vessels into Western countries for financial gain.

It follows that it is possible for antagonists to infiltrate a merchant vessel in a foreign port, at sea, or in territorial waters or a home port with the intention of damaging the port, harming other infrastructure, or transporting a containerized threat inland. Terrorists could work with organized crime or independently. The threat could be physical (collision or blockage), explosive, toxic, or even nuclear or biological.

The traditional openness of the maritime transport system leaves numerous opportunities to be exploited. The increases of piracy and maritime crime on the world's seaways have been well covered by the media. Maritime crimes are surprising by their magnitude: in 2003 pirates staged 454 attacks, continuing a series of annual increases; 311 ships were illegally boarded, and 92 people were confirmed killed or missing.[2] The main areas for piracy are the Malacca Straits and the South China Sea, however, the Horn of Africa and the Caribbean also experience numerous attacks.

For many years, criminals have used the anonymity of maritime transportation for smuggling arms, drugs and illegal immigrants. However, in recent years transnational crime has been joined by, and in some cases linked with, terrorism—a chemistry that drastically increases the threat potential. In early 2003, the chemical tanker *Dewi Madrim*, was hijacked by pirates, who used the ship as a practice platform for learning navigation and pilotage. They also kidnapped officers in order to gain expertise on conducting a maritime attack.[3] A recent maritime threat assessment from the Australian government stated that Al Qaida and its associated groups, Abu Sayyaf in the Philippines and Jemaah Islamiah in Indonesia, "are known to have a capacity to conduct significant terrorist attacks, including against maritime interests."[4] Alexey Muraviev, an Australian security expert, has stated that terrorists have the operational capabilities to mount a terrorist attack at sea. Muriviev notes that these attacks could be on a variety of targets including transport ships, container ships, LNG carriers, chemical carriers, as well as coastal and offshore infrastructure. He states that the attacks can occur by several means such as "by deploying suicide scuba divers, [or] by using sea mines."[5]

There have been two well known terrorist successes against shipping targets: the suicide attack by a small boat on the USS *Cole* that was alongside in Aden in October 2000; and the at-sea attack on a French oil tanker *Limberg* in the Gulf of Aden in October 2002. The small boat attack from sea of a vital Iraqi oil facility in April 2004 signaled a new tactic focused on maritime infrastructure.[6] Moreover, the dual attack on Ashdod Port, Israel in March 2004 by Hamas and Fatah terrorists shows that port facilities can be attacked from land or sea.[7] Both methods have been used recently and therefore are likely to be familiar to modern terrorists for future operations. Moreover, there have been numerous maritime terrorism plots uncovered in the last two years, including the arrest of three Moroccan terrorists who were planning to attack US, British and Israeli ships in the Straits of Gibraltar. As well, the seizure of a ship off Sicily carrying an Al Qaida cell thought to be planning attacks on Italy indicates that terrorists are aware of maritime possibilities.[8] It is well known that Al Qaida itself owns a number of cargo ships, approximately 20 of which are medium- to large-sized vessels capable of reaching North American shores. Closer to North America, in August 2003, US federal prosecutors claimed that Al Qaida "sought to buy access to commercial shipping containers bound from Pakistan for Port Newark."[9] The decision to close down the large

Alaskan port of Valdez when the United States assumed a high security alert level in late December 2003 was an important event. Based on serious warning information, the US Coast Guard acted to protect a *North American port* from attack—either by air or sea.[10] More recently, the US Coast Guard arrested nine Al Qaida terror suspects in the US merchant marine in March 2004.[11]

It is evident from this that terrorists are at sea and active. Although it has not been discovered that Canada's maritime interests have been specifically targeted by Al Qaida or other terrorist groups, the inclusion of "Canadians" as fifth in a prioritized list with Americans, British, Spanish, Australians and Italians as preferred targets in an Al Qaida memorandum in April 2004 proves that Canada is being considered for Al Qaida attacks in general.[12]

Strategic Terrorism: A Change

It is important at this juncture to describe why the terrorism that Al Qaida represents is new and different. It has been stated that "the terrorist changed the battlespace" by coming from nowhere, and striking at civilians using civilian means of transportation as weapons, *but in a strategic, military way*, terrorism has altered the way states think about domestic security.[13] Bruce Berkowitz, an American author and expert on intelligence and terrorism, points out the main features that distinguish the new kind of warfare—referred to as "strategic terrorism." These features include:

1. a global network consisting of small, semi-autonomous cells capable of operating with little centralized control to achieve the strategic goals of the parent organization;
2. the use of unconventional weapons of mass destruction (e.g., hijacked airliners) to cause huge casualties and enormous physical damage and to attract as much publicity as possible;
3. a synergetic alliance between a terrorist network and one or

more authoritarian states ... that provide the network with logistics and funding for its non-attributable army; and

4. information superiority, in both its "soft" (an alluring ideological message to recruit and motivate foot soldiers) and "hard" (secure global communications for logistics, financial support, and command and control) forms.[14]

Most of the terrorist organizations that have come to prominence in the past had a local, tactical focus, exercised restraint in the use of violence and had the desire to end up at a bargaining table of some sort. This is not the case in the current situation. Strategic terrorism is different. According to Jonathan Stevenson,

> Al Qaeda, on the other hand, represents a transnational threat—one very different in kind from that posed by the IRA or even newer groups such as Hamas. Al Qaeda has potentially thousands of members and no interest in bargaining with the United States or its allies. Instead, it seeks to cripple them, by inflicting mass casualties if possible, potentially with weapons of mass destruction.[15]

When one is dealing with the topic of security, three key lessons from 9/11 and its aftermath become clear:

1. The terrorist has found seams in Western organizational structures by striking at the local level but using federal or strategic-level apparatus with strategic aims. The modern terrorist focuses huge destructive power at a local target for maximum sensation;
2. The terrorist owns the time-line in domestic security operations. The onus is on the defending government or governments to disrupt this time-line.
3. Only through mastery of information and swift reaction will prevention of terrorist attacks occur.

Even more worrisome is the "protean nature" of strategic terrorism. Al Qaida, like a chameleon, constantly evolves. And, as Jessica Stern notes, it has shown

> a surprising willingness to adapt its mission. This capacity for change has consistently made the group more appealing to recruits, attracted surprising new allies, and—most worrisome from a Western perspective—made it harder to detect and destroy.[16]

A seaborne terrorist attack could kill thousands of people and cost billions of dollars by causing the closure of one or many major ports in the aftermath. The global maritime trading system has already shown this vulnerability during the western US port labour strikes of 2002. Admiral James Loy, the Deputy Secretary of Homeland Security in the United States observes, "Their [Al Qaida's] ultimate goal is attacking our economy."[17] As recently as September 2004, US intelligence agencies have passed on warnings to allies about a plot to have pirates "hijack an oil tanker or freighter and turn it into a floating bomb" in the choke-point region of the Straits of Malacca.[18] The information was intercepted from communications from Al Qaida affiliate Jemaah Islamiah which revealed that "a new tape either carrying bin Laden or his deputy's message was on its way, and that it was intended to trigger a major terror attack."[19] Thus, the brand of strategic terrorism that Western governments are facing today is truly a strategic, but agile, amorphous and deadly form of warfare that affects the economic, financial, security, military and even political sectors of targeted states.

The new form of warfare known as strategic terrorism, as well as more traditional threats, has the potential to destabilize the international interaction of states. It also has potential to disturb the environment, disrupt internal interaction and threaten human life, including the lives of innocent non-combatants. Moreover, interaction in the maritime environment has been shown to be particularly vulnerable. Since states want to maintain (and improve) their ability to interact in the maritime environment and support maritime linkages, they find themselves challenged to protect what they have set in motion. They desire maritime security.

In order for national governments to respond to this challenge, they have to comprehend the new battlespace and react to its changed shape. Today's terrorist organizations have the ability to attack from many directions, disperse their resources worldwide and use a variety of unconventional tactics to attack targets and evade intelligence and law enforcement bodies. They can "organize themselves in ways that take advantage of geographic, political and bureaucratic boundaries—that is, they often try to slip between the cracks where the authority of one intelligence or law enforcement organization ends and another begins."[20] Moreover, they have adopted a strategy of leaderless organization in which members and groups around the globe operate independently from each other towards a central, common aim. As Stern has noted, "Leaders do not issue orders or pay operatives; instead, they inspire small cells or individuals to take action on their own initiative."[21]

Since the struggle against these threats does not focus on sovereign states in particular, the battlespace becomes a combination of local and federal, domestic and international, sensational and common place. According to Martin Rudner:

> Precisely because of their consuming hatred of the West and its values, their asymmetric deployment of weaponry of mass destruction, their obscure command structure and embedded cellular network, their widespread transnational linkages and self-sacrificing ethos, al-Qaeda and its affiliates present a security threat of exceptional complexity, resilience, and peril to open and democratic societies in Europe and North

America, to ethnically plural developing countries in East Africa and Asia, and to the established authorities in the Arab and Muslim lands.[22]

It is clear that, like guerrilla warriors, terrorists own and control the time-line for their operations—it is up to non-terrorists to disrupt that time-line and prevent the mission from being achieved. Since the battlespace is informational and ephemeral, it is not through overpowering physical means that states will neutralize the threat. It is through information superiority and the agility to react that the threat will be neutralized. To prevent a terrorist event in this battlespace, governments will have to depend more on brains than on brawn.

Government Response

Many Western governments have acted to respond to this complex threat. The complexity, leaderlessness and protean nature of the threat forces governments to look at new ways in which to use their security machinery. The balance between security and civil liberties that was set up in the Cold War years which "combines organizational distinctions with constitutional protections with restraints on official discretion" will no longer always suffice in its present form.[23] Strategic terrorism compels a rethinking of this balance. This means that governments have had to re-evaluate how they interact with other governments and government departments and rethink how they relate to each other, the constitution and the citizenry. Since terrorism is defined as a crime as well as a national security threat in most jurisdictions, the various cultures that exist in the fabric of government departments find themselves being induced to support each other more closely than ever before—sometimes against their nature. Consequently, the government functions that evolved in most countries during the Cold War years—i.e., organizational stovepipes that focused on compartmentalized areas of government interest—are in the midst of a re-evaluation of how they should interact with others to achieve their aims.

Governments have four major functional areas relating to national security:

- law enforcement;
- intelligence;
- infrastructure protection; and
- defence.

The departments which share responsibility for these functional areas each have legislated mandates that bestow a certain specific authority to carry out their tasks. Thus, in the past, law enforcement agencies often worked independently from security intelligence agencies; the military often concentrated on external threats and rarely met with departments with domestic concerns; and infrastructure protection or health officials often worked in isolation ensuring that their specific tasks were successfully achieved. Government organization for maritime security was no different. Individual fleets of government ships put to sea under separate mandates, surveillance over large ocean spaces was often largely uncoordinated with other government agencies, and collaboration took place in reaction to specific activities (usually criminal) that were already underway.

We have seen that modern terrorism defies this convenient compartmentalization of the security framework. Terrorists seek out gaps and seams in traditional government organizations in order to infiltrate and violate. In so doing, terrorism is having the effect of reshaping the response that governments use to counter its attacks. Governments have been forced to break down their traditional stovepipes and integrate their capability. Bruce Berkowitz argues that:

To detect these new threats, one must collect information from a variety of sources that are likely to vary over time. To analyze these data, one must share the available facts with as many experts as possible and hope someone sees the pattern—"connects the dots," to use the recent parlance.[24]

Efforts to protect facilities, plans for surveillance of approaches to borders and capability for coordinated reaction to threats all lead to an overlapping of the traditional government divisions. Government organizations need to become "agile" in order to adapt to a constantly changing threat.[25] An example of this sort of response is the government of Prime Minister John Howard in Australia. After a number of years (before and after 9/11) dealing with the threat of organized crime and terrorism, the government concluded that an integrated, "whole-of-government" approach was necessary.[26] Yet, such change is not easily or quickly accomplished. In addition to overcoming inevitable bureaucratic inertia and outright resistance, all democratic governments who are reacting to this call to collaborate for security will be faced with strident objections from those who are entrusted with protecting civil liberties. This is a debate in which each country must engage in order to achieve a balance that is right for itself.

In response to the blurring of functional lines by the terrorist, the functional divisions of government are being altered and reshaped to deal with the new reality. It is no longer sufficient to depend on the traditional functional lines that governments have utilized. Militaries are cooperating more closely with law enforcers who are in turn working more closely with intelligence agencies under the rubric of national security.

Instead of using traditional functional lines in government, this research will examine methods of responding—i.e., the activities required for response—to the post-9/11 battlespace. In order to draw out key factors that illuminate how each case-country prioritizes its approach to maritime security, the government activities of collaboration, domain awareness, safeguarding and responsiveness will be utilized. It is worth noting that in each of these activity areas, government departments can participate together or apart inside the sphere of maritime security. They also permit cooperation at different levels of government such as national, international, local or regional. By using these key factors, government departments and foreign governments can combine efforts in areas where the terrorist furtively schemes. As always, however, governments and their agents are limited by constitutional laws that ensure their activities do not jeopardize human rights and civil liberties.

The intention here is to use these four key maritime security activities (collaboration, domain awareness, safeguarding and responsiveness) to illustrate the practices and approaches to maritime security of the case-countries so that these approaches can be interpreted and assessed. By applying these key activities to the case-countries and prioritizing them in order of importance in each country, the most important approaches will become evident. Once all three case-countries have been analysed, the list of best practices derived from a comparison of all three approaches will enable us to draw conclusions about the selection of national responses to challenges in maritime security.

Notes

1. Stefano Ambrogi, "Al Qaida plans to Target Merchant Shipping," in an interview with Admiral Sir Alan West in Gibraltar to *Lloyds List Maritime Newspaper* (5 August 2004). Available from http://www.google.ca/search?q=cache:P190yJk6yGEJ:www.reuters.com/newsArticle.jhtml%3Ftype%3DworldNews%26storyID%3D5885193+Ambrogi+Al+Qaeda+West&hl=en (Cited 15 September 2004).
2. John Kerin, "Navy Shifts from Battles to Piracy," *The Australian*

(6 February 2004). Available from http://www.theaustralian. news.com.au/printpage/0,5942,8596760,00.html (Cited 15 September 2004).

3. Joseph Fara, "Al-Qaida Plans High-sea Terror," *Joseph Farah's G2 Bulletin* (13 October 2003). Available from http:// worldnetdaily.com/news/article.asp?ARTICLE_ID=35047 (Cited 15 September 2004).

4. Australia, Attorney General. Statement issued by the Office of the Australia's Attorney General to Cargo Security International on 30 April 2004. Available from http://www.cargosecurity international.com/print.asp?id=2579 (Cited 15 September 2004).

5. Alexey Muraviev, "Expert Issues Maritime Security Warning," ABC Online website (29 March 2004). Interview with Alison Caldwell. Available from http://www.abc.net.au/pm/content/2004/ s1076558.htm (Cited 15 September 2004).

6. Matthew Fisher, "Insurgents attack Iraqi Oil Facilities," *The Ottawa Citizen,* 25 April 2004, sec. A1.

7. Israeli Ministry of Foreign Affairs, "Suicide bombing at Ashdod Port," Israeli Ministry of Foreign Affairs website (14 March 2004). Available from http://www.mfa.gov.il/MFA/MFAArchive/ 2000_2009/2004/3/ Suicide+bombing+at+Ashdod+Port+14-Mar-2004.htm (Cited 15 September 2004).

8. Tim Weiner, "World Ports Struggle to Meet U.S. Security Standards," *The International Herald Tribune,* 25 March 2004, sec. A2.

9. *Ibid.*

10. Zaz Hollander and Wesley Loy, "Valdez Tanker Port Shut Down," *The Anchorage Daily News,* 1 January 2004.

11. Caroline Drees, "U.S. Probe Spots 9 Terror Suspects in Merchant Marine," *Wired News* (4 March 2004). Available from http:// www.worldaffairsboard.com/showthread.php?t=1738 (Cited 15 September 2004).

12. Lisa Meyers, "Memo Outlines al-Qaida Terror Plans," *NBC News* (1 April 2004). Available from http://www.msnbc.msn.com/id/ 4647682/ (Cited 15 September 2004).

13. Avis, "Surveillance and Canadian Maritime Domestic Security," p. 9.

14. Berkowitz, "Intelligence and the War on Terrorism," p. 289.

15. Jonathan Stevenson, "How Europe and America Defend Themselves," *Foreign Affairs*, Vol. 82, No. 2 (March/April 2003), p. 79.
16. Jessica Stern, "The Protean Enemy," *Foreign Affairs*, Vol. 82, No. 4 (July/August 2003), p. 28.
17. Weiner, "World Ports Struggle to Meet U.S. Security Standards," A2.
18. Phillip Sherwell, Massoud Ansari and Marianne Kearney, "Al Qa'eda terrorists plan to turn tanker into a floating bomb," *The Telegraph (UK)*. Available from http://www.telegraph.co.uk/news/main.jhtml?xml=/ news/2004/09/12/wterr12.xml (Cited 18 September 2004).
19. *Ibid.*
20. Berkowitz, "Intelligence and the War on Terrorism," p. 292.
21. Stern, "The Protean Enemy," p. 34.
22. Rudner, "Hunters and Gatherers," p. 221.
23. Gregory Treverton, "Balancing Security and Liberty in the War on Terror." Available from http://www.maxwell.syr.edu/campbell/Library%20Papers/Event%20papers/ISHS/Treverton.pdf (Cited 15 September 2004).
24. Berkowitz, "Spying in the Post September 11 World," p. 3.
25. *Ibid.*
26. John Howard, "Strategic Leadership for Australia: Policy Directions in a Complex World," speech delivered by Prime Minister Howard at the meeting of the Committee for Economic Development Australia, Canberra, 20 November, 2002, p. ii.

CHAPTER 3
CASE STUDY, AUSTRALIA

Overview: Maritime Perspective

An island continent, Australia has no contiguous neighbours nor does it have a major state power in its immediate vicinity. The landmass of Australia is just slightly smaller than that of mainland USA, yet its coastline measures 25,760 kilometres.[1] A notable geographic feature is the absence of any large river systems, like the St. Lawrence River, that link the interior of Australia to the coastal urban centres. While the southern approaches to the continent are sparsely navigated, the northern approaches are inundated with maritime traffic through the strategically significant Strait of Malacca and South China Sea trade routes as well as the Torres Strait which narrowly separates Australia from neighbouring Indonesia and Papua New Guinea. Australia has 300 port facilities, however, only 70 of these are considered large enough ports to have significant security concerns.[2] With a Gross National Product of $528 billion in 2003 (compared to Canada's $923 billion), Australia depends on unimpeded maritime waterways and port facilities in order to take advantage of a valuable $180 billion (USD) maritime trade in mining and agricultural goods which account for 57% of Australia's goods and services exports.[3] Australia generates 12% of the world's shipping tasks.[4]

Australia traditionally depended on British and then American maritime protection in the South Pacific region. As Tewes, Rayner and Kavanaugh noted, "Australia's size, its isolation, sparse population and limited financial resources have made security difficult to even contemplate achieving alone, however, although reducing the feeling of vulnerability, this reliance on allies has tended to inhibit the development of strategic independence."[5] The latter half of the 1990s witnessed a more assertive stance by the Australian government to secure its own national and regional interests as well as a desire to participate in the larger strategic maritime environment.

Since the 1940s, Australia has grown in population from seven million to 20 million people, welcoming over six million immigrants in that time. Of Australians that were born overseas in 2001, approximately 40% are from non-Western countries (North Africa and the Middle East 12%, Asia 12%, Oceania 11%, the Americas 4%, and Sub-Saharan Africa 3.5%).[6] This aggressive migration program has become more tightly controlled regarding entrance criteria in the last decade.

National Security Developments

Like all countries in the West, the national security policy of the Australian government has evolved steadily through the last decade. Australia's unique strategic circumstances have meant security policy has blended traditional concerns over immigration into a national security campaign focused on anti-terrorism. The government has placed national security as its top national priority and completely re-shaped its wide-ranging security apparatus.[7] This restructuring effort by the Howard government foresaw the changed "battlespace" of international terrorism and its links to organized crime.

Following the recommendations of several well-focused Parliamentary Committees, the government used far-reaching legislative changes to enable collaboration in both horizontal and vertical directions—alterations seen as requirements of the changing security environment. Thus, the existing Australian governmental security system has a logical flow of responsibility and coordination. It starts at the regional and state level in the various interagency operations centres, intelligence collection agencies and law enforcement units. It moves from there to the federal level through departmental routes to interdepartmental centres (such as the National Surveillance Centre). It then combines all appropriate national agencies with regional representatives horizontally and vertically in national committees—including blended input from both law enforcement and intelligence bodies (as one finds in the National Counter-Terrorism Committee). Finally, the security system engages in national policy in a "whole-of-government" approach which combines national security with international input (in the National Security Committee of Cabinet). The unifying legislation that was passed in Australia allows for seamless horizontal and vertical collaboration between federal and regional government entities for a common cause. Thus, Australia has created governmental machinery which allows the Prime Minister to act quite freely with respect to national security concerns.

One must keep in mind that there are many critics of this overall approach. As elsewhere, there are critics who feel that democracy and civil liberties have been overly sacrificed in the march to national security.

It should be noted that the "whole-of-government" approach just described is very different from the US approach to 'Homeland Security' which created a whole new bureaucratic structure after 9/11.[8] Australia's system evolved throughout the last decade taking care of issues that were unique to an island continent in the South Pacific. As well, as Malcolm Brailey notes, "The small size of Australian government institutions, and the co-location of all senior officers and politicians in Canberra, facilitates direct communication within government."[9] The security solution reflects an attempt to meet Australian needs with distinctly Australian solutions.

Within this unique Australian governmental framework, maritime security policy and structure has evolved at a similar quick pace. Although Australia does not have a formal maritime strategy (as many other middle power countries, including Canada, do not), the most recent White Paper on defence manages to enunciate strategic maritime policy which breaks away from the traditional military-dominated, defence-oriented approach. According to Tewes et al:

> *Defence 2000* ... was the first White Paper to recognize that controlling our sea and air approaches was a joint operation and that maritime forces included all three services. Compared to previous policies, the White Paper clearly recognized the role of maritime forces in maritime security of the wider region, the protection of Australian ports from sea mines, support of civil law enforcement and coastal surveillance operations.[10]

In the maritime context then, this policy laid the foundation for the military to join the whole-of-government approach. As a middle power, Australia could not aspire to full command of the sea like its American allies in the post-Cold War era. Instead, the Australian government focused on combining what resources and capabilities it possessed in order to protect Australia's interests. The government worked to "bring together the elements of such power in such a way to maintain their ability to use the sea to achieve their national interests."[11] 'Power' here does not just mean military power, but the full spectrum of national power that a state has at its disposal.

The prime example of this economical usage of government resources is found in Australia's solution for maritime surveillance and border security. Instead of forming a Coast Guard, the federal Department of Justice and Customs was given the responsibility to deliver an effective civil maritime surveillance and response service. It was named Customs Coastwatch. An overhaul in 1999 resulted in an influx of new resources to Coastwatch such as new aircraft, trained staff and a National Surveillance Centre that combined the existing operational and planning capability of the interdepartmental staff with a much-needed analytical role.[12] In the years 2000-2001, illegal immigrants and people-smuggling via boat were at a peak, so the Howard government moved for greater integration of the Australian Defence Force (ADF) into home security.[13] Coastwatch welcomed a Rear-Admiral from the ADF as its head and it incorporated naval staff as well as specially-designed naval patrol vessels and aircraft into an otherwise Customs Department-mandated operation. Furthermore, its activities are dependent on the reports of the surveillance and response needs of its major clients in an interdepartmental context from the regions (fisheries, immigration, health, transport, environment, federal and regional police, and customs). Although these changes ushered in improvements, they led to significant criticism from human rights groups and the media that the treatment of refugees and migrants was too harsh.

Prioritizing Approaches to Maritime Security

Limited resources vis-a-vis the security challenge means that every state must adopt a method of prioritization so that vulnerability gaps can be filled according to their importance. Like other Western states in the post-9/11 world, the Australian government has had to undertake both strategic and tactical responses to improve the security of ships, ports, territorial and coastal waterways, offshore exploitation activities, international waters, and national interests in foreign waters and ports.

In order to determine Australian priorities in the new security environment, the four maritime security activities discussed earlier—collaboration, domain awareness, safeguarding and responsiveness—will be utilized as key factors. The use of certain tools in each of these activity areas such as resource allocation, changes to machinery of government, amendments to legislation, policy development, information sharing, changes to intelligence organization mandates, and the establishment of warning and assessment capability will serve as indicators of importance in the whole-government prioritization process.

Government reaction to the threats of illegal migration and people-smuggling through organized crime in the 1990s laid the foundation for further security initiatives in the face of international terrorism after 9/11 and Bali. Focusing on the Sydney Olympics in 2000, the recommendations of the Joint Committee on the National Crime Authority helped the government to select its top priority for improving maritime security—the enabling activity of collaboration. When asked to prioritize Australian security activities, Coastwatch officials unanimously chose collaboration as the top priority of government, even though their surveillance specialty might have led to a bias for domain awareness in top position.[14] According to Group Captain Ian Pearson,

> Due to legislative freedom worked out through the last five years, interdepartmental groups (I will use maritime people-smuggling as the example), which include defence, immigration, customs, national and regional police, ASIO and ASIS, and foreign affairs, work very closely. Sharing is top-notch.[15]

Collaboration
The realization that international terrorists and criminals seek to operate between the seams of governing organizations led the Howard government to adopt collaboration as the foundation of its national security effort. In its final report of 1997, the Joint Committee on the National Crime Authority made a landmark recommendation which set the reform in motion. The recommen-

dation was that "the Australian Government take steps to ensure there are no legislative barriers which would inhibit the free flow of information and intelligence between security and law enforcement agencies."[16] The government "accepted the principles underpinning" this recommendation and went on to form Australia's "whole-of-government approach" based on the underlying ideas.[17]

The National Security Committee of Cabinet (NSCC) embodies this approach at the highest level. The legislated ability of all three intelligence agencies—the Australian Security Intelligence Organization (ASIO), the Australian Secret Intelligence Service (ASIS) and the Defence Security Department (DSD)—to cooperate with each other and with police agencies through the NSCC, the National Counter-Terrorism Committee (NCTC) and subordinate committees under the *Intelligence Services Act 2001*, helps to avoid the "silo-syndrome" that the United States and UK have suffered, and leads to earlier alerting of enforcement agencies.[18]

The Leaders' Summit on Terrorism and Multi-jurisdictional Crime in 2002 was a landmark gathering which aided in closing seams between *levels* of government. The state and territory Attorneys-General agreed to pass legislation to refer constitutional power to the Commonwealth (federal government) in "national terrorist situations."[19] The leaders also agreed to

> improve Australia's anti-terrorist intelligence capacity and to develop effective means for sharing intelligence …[and] upgrade the central coordination capacity so that the operational arms of the Commonwealth and the States and the Territories can obtain information and strategic advice necessary to respond rapidly and effectively.[20]

The Australian whole-of-government approach laid the foundation for national security, and thus maritime security, in legislation that ensured "that information of a preventative nature is freely distributed between relevant agencies, *even to the point of removing legislative barriers* to such free exchange."[21]

The second collaborative approach of interest is the Common Risk-Assessment Methodology (CRAM) that was recommended to the Coastwatch organization by the Australian National Audit Office. Regional centres collect their intelligence and make recommendations according to a common system three months prior to when the federal decision to deploy resources is made. In this way, the federal resource managers can compare assessments across the country that are based on the same timeframe and meet optimum requirements for a certain prescribed period. The information can also be compared with other regions, assessed against intelligence for probability of occurrence, weighed for economic, social and environmental severity, and assigned a common risk score. This approach ensures that regional centres, that vie for resource allocation, speak the same language to federal resource managers by judging threats with a common numerical standard.[22] From these reports, the central authority in Customs Coastwatch can mete out the air and sea resources according to intelligence assessments of the future threat from its various government partners.

Outside national borders, the collaborative approach is integrated into Australian agreements with neighbouring countries and international organizations. The government worked through the Association of Southeast Asian Nations (ASEAN) to initiate and sign a number of bilateral Memoranda of Understanding on counter-terrorism with regional counterparts in Singapore, Fiji, Indonesia, Malaysia, Thailand, South Korea and the Philippines. These understandings will include the placement of Australian transport, federal police and Australian Security Intelligence Organization (ASIO) officers in regional embassies to provide assistance. This has given the Australian government a valuable window into the strengths and weaknesses of its regional partners with respect to security, an opportunity to assist these governments, and a potential early warning capability.

Domain Awareness

The most visible tool that the Australian government utilizes from its maritime security toolbox is domain awareness. The aircraft and vessels of Coastwatch are on the front lines of this "civil surveillance" activity and are often the face of maritime security in the media. According to Group Captain Pearson, "domain awareness places a close second to collaboration in priority due to the Australian belief in strong border control."[23] What makes Australia's approach to domain awareness different from other countries is its heavy emphasis on *civilian air contract services*. To achieve an impressive 90 per cent surveillance coverage rate[24] in the most vulnerable areas of the north and northwest, Coastwatch utilizes a fleet of leased, fixed-wing civilian aircraft, helicopters (specifically for the Torres Strait), and supporting maritime patrol aircraft from the Australian Defence Force. Seventeen leased aircraft are employed on 4,500 surveillance flights annually to cover 392 million square kilometres. These air resources are backed up by a developing radar satellite system (RADARSAT) and signals intelligence (SIGINT) on all coasts. There is also a supplementary surveillance and presence capability derived from customs and navy patrol vessels.

The radar picture and accompanying information collected from each of these platforms is transferred electronically to the National Surveillance Centre in Canberra. In this second domain awareness approach, the information is analysed, relevant client agencies are consulted, and then necessary follow-up action is directed downwards to the appropriate regional centre. Resources are scheduled three months ahead based on client assessments; however, adjustments are made to meet contingency requirements. Aircraft are used to maintain the picture while a customs vessel or navy patrol boat executes the response. This approach then utilizes a system of regional coordination centres that spans across the continent, which passes information and assessments upwards and receives direction from the officials at the National Surveillance Centre. By connecting the regional centres to the national centre and clarifying the command structure through legislation, the Australian levels of government have been able to centralize and standardize their coordinated surveillance effort.

To supplement geo-spatial surveillance data, foreign intelligence is gathered and disseminated to mandated clients within the system. Australia's overseas intelligence collection agency, Australian Secret Intelligence Service (ASIS), adds the foreign human intelligence that is crucially important for identifying terrorist or criminal suspects before they arrive in Australia. This information is fed into the tightly controlled Travel Entry/Exit Data Base that is maintained by Customs and Immigration. Because Australia is an island, the only points of exit and entry are seaports and airports; therefore, every single ingress and egress is tracked for the continent through time.[25] Other departments may enquire on a case-by-case basis for this information based on the *Customs Act.* Responsible to the government through the Minister of Foreign Affairs, ASIS obtains intelligence in response to priorities determined by key agencies such as the Office of National Assessments (ONA), the Department of the Prime Minister and Cabinet, the Department of Foreign Affairs, and the Department of Defence.[26] The *Intelligence Services Act 2001* gives ASIS the mandate to function secretly in the interests of Australia's national security, foreign relations and economic well-being. ASIS adds valuable information to the strategic picture and shares its foreign intelligence with its maritime security counterparts and the Office of National Assessments.

Safeguarding
The third priority for Australian maritime security is the activity of safeguarding ports, vessels and waterways. Just as most states

in the international system have striven to meet the International Maritime Organization's (IMO) new security regime embodied in the International Ship and Port Facility Security (ISPS) Code, Australia has been able to achieve the required level of security planning on time. Australia's *Maritime Transport Security Act 2003* includes the IMO directives and provides the legislative basis for requiring industry and port authorities to comply to the standards promulgated therein. While Al Qaida has stated its intent to attack Australian interests and is known to have the capability to carry out maritime attacks, ASIO has assessed that the threat to ports and shipping is low to very low in most cases, although there are some areas that have been assessed as a medium threat.[27]

Based on these assessments, the government has chosen an indirect approach to bolster port and ship security. Instead of passing direct funding to port authorities, which are a mixture of private and state-owned agencies, the government increased funding to the federal Customs Department on 12 May 2004.[28] These additional funds will enable customs officers to board all first-time vessels to Australian ports, to carry out random checks of other vessels, to monitor 56 port areas and 88 wharves around the clock via closed-circuit television (CCTV), and to increase the flying hours of Coastwatch surveillance aircraft. Following the successful start-up of the ISPS code in all Australian ports, the X-ray inspection of containers in major ports is to be increased to five per cent (in line with Canada and the United States), closed-circuit cameras doubled, a task force created to review security arrangements for offshore platforms, and security identification cards for maritime industry employees introduced.[29] Nevertheless, the government has deferred any mention of funding to assist port authorities until an independent review is completed.[30] Without an additional $300M to implement the new international security plans, it is unlikely that the desired physical security measures will be in place for quite some time.

A second safeguarding approach sees the use of bilateral agreements between Australia and its closest regional trading partners. This set of agreements allows Australia to assist developing states in the region in forming their security systems and has the added advantage of learning lessons from them, a novel approach for a middle power (the United States does this frequently). This effort is facilitated by the generous contribution of over $1M (Australian dollars) to each of the regional partners through the Transport Department-sponsored AUSAID fund to help the various governments meet the IMO deadline as well as improve overall regional security.

Responsiveness
The final priority of the four activities for maritime security and intelligence in Australia is responsiveness. The Director of Operations at Coastwatch explains:

> There is recognition that response is essential for maritime security. However, only small waterborne resources shared between Navy and Customs provide this capability. Response is an essential part of the Coastwatch mandate; yet there are still resource gaps that impede speedy reaction and enforcement. They are limited in reaction capability on the water— large area, few assets.[31]

There are eight sea-going customs vessels of the National Marine Unit that provide the main thrust of responsiveness at sea. This resource level is low for the challenge.

A controversial approach taken recently by the Howard government is the legislated capability of ASIO (under the *Australian Security Intelligence Organization (ASIO) Legislation Amendment (Terrorism) Act 2002*) to exercise its powers to question and detain persons who are suspected of having information relevant to a terrorist offence. This implies that ASIO has the legal right to detain and question Australians and foreigners in Australia based only on intelligence that the detainee has information pertaining to a terrorist offence. This has been challenged by human rights and legal groups as a step too far and will be appealed when the sunset clause is activated in 2006.

Finally, the effort that the Australian government has put into a "national security campaign" should be mentioned with regard to responsiveness. Australia has a National Alert System which has been at level Medium since 9/11. In December 2002, a public education campaign started which included television and radio advertising, a national security website (which still exists), a National Security Hotline, and many booklets with additional information at the household level. The public education campaign was completed in 2003, with only a lukewarm response across the country. Nevertheless, the Alert System, the website, and the hotline are seen as very useful windows into the national security system and allow for input from the public which could be crucial to responding to a national security threat.

Conclusion

The 10-year evolution of Australia's security and intelligence system stemmed from Australia's unique security situation. It is a testament to the continuity of Australia's government that such unifying policy development was able to occur, particularly after the events of 11 September. The approaches that the Australian government has chosen to adopt for increased maritime security are a product of a continuous government vision that seeks to address the unique challenges of Australia's strategic situation. The high importance placed on collaboration and domain awareness stems from an early and comprehensive understanding of the new global threat as well as a profound appreciation for the particular geographic and strategic position in which Australia finds itself. Compared to other countries' approaches, which stem from different strategic priorities, several of these approaches will rise above the others as best practices that can be considered particularly useful for governments wishing to improve their maritime security policy in the altered threat environment.

Notes

1. "Australia Geography – 2003," *The World Factbook 2004*, updated 11 May 2004. Available from http://www.theodora.com/wfb2003/australia/australia_geography.html (Cited 15 September 2004).
2. John Hirst, Executive Director of Australian Ports and Marine Authorities Association, "Ports 'Vulnerable,' Marine Authority Says," *ABC News Online* (22 March 2004). Available from http://www.abc.net.au/news/newsitems/s1071093.htm (Cited 15 September 2004).
3. US Department of State, "Australia Background Notes," US Department of State website.
4. John Anderson, Australia's Minister of Transport, in an interview in Sydney for *The Age* newspaper, 21 March 2004. Available from http://www.theage.com.au/articles/2004/03/21/1079823236334.html (Cited 15 September 2004).
5. Tewes, Rayner and Kavanaugh, "A Foundation Paper on Australia's Maritime Strategy," p. 2.
6. Australia Department of Immigration, "Australian Immigration Fact Sheet," Australia Department of Immigration website. Available from http://www.immi.gov.au/facts/04fifty.htm (Cited 15 September 2004).
7. Howard, "Strategic Leadership for Australia: Policy Directions in a Complex World," p. iii.
8. For a discussion of the differences see Malcolm Brailey, "Australia's Approach to 'Homeland Security,'" in *Institute of Defense and Strategic Studies (IDSS) Commentaries* (August 2003), p. 2. Available from http://www.ntu.edu.sg/idss/Perspective/research_050330.htm (Cited 15 September 2004).

9. *Ibid.*
10. Tewes, Rayner and Kavanaugh, "A Foundation Paper on Australia's Maritime Strategy," p. 13.
11. *Ibid.*, p. 15.
12. "Overview of Customs Coastwatch," *The Australian Journal of Emergency Management*, Vol. 18, No. 3 (August 2003), p. 4.
13. Group Captain Ian Pearson, Director of Australian Coastwatch Operations, phone interview by author, Ottawa/Canberra, 7 May 2004.
14. Interviews of Australian officials by the author (Group Captain Pearson, Mr. Tom Anderson, Lieutenant Commander Richard Davies), Ottawa/Canberra, May-July 2004.
15. Group Captain Ian Pearson interview. ASIS is the Australian Secret Intelligence Service and ASIO is the Australian Security Intelligence Organization.
16. Australia, Parliamentary Joint Committee on the National Crime Authority, Hearings on National Crime Authority: Mr. Raymond Kendall, Secretary General of Interpol (Canberra, December, 1996), p. 8. Available from http://www.aph.gov.au/hansard/joint/commttee/j5963242.pdf (Cited 15 September 2004).
17. Australia, Parliamentary Joint Committee on the National Crime Authority, *Annual Report 1996-1997* (Canberra, September 1997), paragraph 45. Available from http://www.aph.gov.au/Senate/committee/acc_ctte/annual/1996/report2/contents.htm (Cited 15 September 2004).
18. Malcolm Farr, "This is Another Cold War," *The Daily Telegraph*, 6 May 2004, p. 4.
19. Australia, Prime Minister's Office, *Commonwealth and States and Territories Agreement on Terrorism and Multi-jurisdictional Crime* (Canberra, April 2002), p. 1. Available from http://www.nationalsecurity.gov.au/agd/www/rwpattach.nsf/viewasattachmentpersonal/(2A296B295C1E058B328FED2164E40B7D)~IGA+as+at+22+October.doc/$file/IGA+as+at+22+October.doc (Cited 15 September 2004).
20. *Ibid.*
21. Australia, Parliamentary Joint Committee on the National Crime Authority, Hearings on National Crime Authority, Kendall testi-

mony, p. 8. Italics were added to highlight Kendall's idea of altering legislation to enable increased sharing of information between the two security cultures.

22. "Overview of Customs Coastwatch," p. 7.

23. Group Captain Ian Pearson interview.

24. *Ibid.*

25. Tom Anderson, Director of Enforcement Operations Australia Customs, phone interview by author, Ottawa/Canberra, 19 May 2004.

26. Australian Secret Intelligence Service, *The Australian Secret Intelligence Service (ASIS), Information* (Canberra, March 2004), p. 1. Available from http://www.asis.gov.au/about.html (Cited 16 September 2004).

27. Cargo Security International, "Release of maritime threat assessment: Australia's shipping and port infrastructure," Cargo Security International website (30 April 2004). Available from http://www.cargosecurityinternational.com/print.asp (Cited 16 September 2004).

28. Tom Anderson, Director of Enforcement Operations Australia Customs, second phone interview Ottawa/Canberra, 15 June 2004.

29. "Al-Qeada at Heart of Port Action," News.com.au website (2 September 2004). Available from http://www.news.com.au/common/story_page/0,4057,10191215%255E1702,00.html (Cited 16 September 2004).

30. Alison Caldwell, "Port Authorities demand funding for security measures," ABC Online website (22 March 2004). Available from http://www.abc.net.au/pm/content/2004/s1071335.htm (Cited 16 September 2004).

31. Group Captain Ian Pearson interview.

CHAPTER 4
CASE STUDY, NETHERLANDS

Overview: Maritime Perspective

Compared to the other countries discussed here, the Netherlands has a very limited coastline. However, it is located at the mouths of three major European rivers—the Rhine, the Meuse and the Schelde—and borders the North Sea. Thus, the Dutch find themselves in a position of maritime confluence for Western Europe and, because of the country's small size and extremely dense population, largely preoccupied with space and volume management both at sea and on land. A large percentage of the surface area of the Netherlands is below sea level, a rare characteristic which leaves it vulnerable to flooding and water-management issues. It has only 451 kilometres of coastline contiguous to the North Sea, but boasts two very large ports on its canal and river systems—Rotterdam, the world's largest container seaport and Amsterdam, the country's capital. The flow of international sea-going merchant traffic is extremely dense as it exits and enters the English Channel and passes through the Dutch exclusive economic zone (EEZ) headed to and from major North Sea German ports, ports in the Baltic Sea and Scandinavian ports to the north.

Positioned as one of the major European transportation hubs, the Netherlands combines its own 635 merchant ships with those of other countries to transport cargo to and from its ports, all of which have superior inter-modal transport connections. The Netherlands derives more than two-thirds of its GDP from merchandise and services trade through a prosperous and open economy which depends heavily on foreign trade.[1]

The Netherlands is Western Europe's largest natural gas producer with 160, or one-third, of its platforms offshore. It also has an expanding offshore oil industry.[2] With a healthy per capita GDP of $28,600 (2003), the Netherlands has a positive balance of trade. Utilizing its strategic position as a transportation hub, it exports $253 billion (USD) worth of industrially processed goods like agricultural products, processed food, chemicals, refined fuels and electrical machinery annually.[3] At the heart of the Dutch inter-modal hub is the container port which handles cargo for much of Europe to and from foreign trading partners. The Dutch Antilles are also a security concern for the Netherlands where it has a Coast Guard Centre and Military Headquarters to carry out primarily law enforcement duties.

The Dutch generally pursue their foreign policy interests, and in particular the fight against international terrorism, through the framework of multilateral organizations. They are loyal members of the United Nations and the European Union as well as numerous other organizations such as the Organization for Security and Cooperation in Europe (OSCE), the Organization of Economic Cooperation and Development (OECD), and the World Trade Organization (WTO). The Netherlands is unique in its longstanding tradition of legal scholarship which makes it the suitable home of the International Court of Justice, the International Criminal Court, and the European police organization EUROPOL. For defence and traditional security matters, the Dutch primarily rely on their membership in NATO and the integration of their national military forces into that alliance.

National Security Developments

To understand the Dutch vision for national and maritime security, one must first place it within the security framework of the European Union. As all land borders are completely open for movement of people and goods, it is the air and sea borders that are looked to for control of ingress and egress.[4] The Netherlands has been a strong proponent of European integration, and most aspects of foreign, economic and trade policies are coordinated through the European Union. However, it must be borne in mind that in the European Union (EU), security is the sovereign responsibility of individual member-states. Looking inward, the EU can seem quite nation-like with its ability to create community policy for its member-states. However, looking outward, the EU remains a hydra with separate Foreign Ministers and many independent and conflicting approaches to national security. Currently there is no single European body that deals with port and maritime security. Thus, each country must struggle not only with its own adaptation to the new threat scenario but also with an unfocused community approach to the same problems on the continental scale.

While the EU is struggling to improve its composite security capability, there are other multilateral organizations like NATO which factor into the European response. At NATO's Prague Summit in November 2002, Heads of State of the member countries adopted a group of measures that were designed to strengthen NATO's preparedness across the spectrum of security challenges, including terrorism and weapons of mass destruction. A very useful focus on defence against weapons of mass destruction includes deployable analytical laboratories, event response teams, an excellence centre, defence stockpiles and disease surveillance systems.[5] But NATO has recently undergone a marked enlargement, it is reconsidering its overall mission, and it has not increased its civilian budget more than four per cent in the last 10 years.[6] The ability to interact with civilian law enforcement agencies in national security issues is likely to progress slowly due to these pressures. As Stevenson notes, "NATO therefore cannot be expected to make much of a contribution to counter-terrorism very soon."[7]

In the Netherlands, the existing government framework includes a Federal Ministerial Crisis Policy Council, supported by an Interdepartmental Policy Team, and fed by a National Coordination Centre, Provincial Coordination Centres and Regional/ Local Coordination Centres. There is not one specific authority for combating terrorism or ensuring maritime security. Thus, the lead department for counter-terrorism, since the focus is acting against criminals, is the Ministry of Justice. For non-criminal events, the Ministry of the Interior or the Ministry of Transport, Public Works and Water Management becomes the lead department depending on the issue. Other departments, including Defence, support the lead agencies. In this shared system of responsibility, "specific elements of response may benefit from even better definition, leaving less room for difference in interpretation regarding authority and responsibility."[8] While the goal is "to achieve an integrated system of cooperative governance" in international, ministerial and operational forums, the effectiveness is often strained by limitations that are beyond the government's control.[9]

Internal threats present unique problems for Dutch authorities. The Netherlands is a country that for several decades has founded its future prosperity on welcoming immigrants from Morocco, Dutch Antilles, Surinam and Turkey. Moreover, it has always strongly espoused the free movement of goods and people across sovereign borders within the EU. Nonetheless, the Netherlands has become more restrictive in its immigration laws dealing with refugees and visa application in the last two years due to concerns of overcrowding and unrest in urban centres. In his seminal article on counter-terrorism in the Netherlands which he presented to the Dutch Parliament in fall of 2003, Eric Akerboom, the Director Democratic Legal Order of the General Intelligence and Security Service (AIVD), came to a difficult conclusion for the Dutch to accept. He noted that:

At the moment we can conclude that the threat of violence represented by Islamist terrorism is growing into a substantial and permanent exogenous *and* endogenous threat. We have been painfully confronted with the fact that also some Muslims raised in the Netherlands are receptive to radical-Islamist ideas and manipulation.[10]

It is worth noting that since the brutal murder of Theo Van Gogh, the famous artist's great-grandson, in late 2004, there has been strain to the breaking point between the Netherlands government and the Muslim population.

In the past, the Dutch Penal Code was found to be wanting in prosecution cases against terrorist suspects. As a result, on 22 June 2004 the Dutch government adopted the Bill on Crimes of Terrorism that made "recruitment of fighters for the Islamic armed struggle or jihad and conspiracy with the intent to commit a serious act of terrorism" separate, punishable criminal offences and increased lengths of existing sentences.[11] Furthermore, conspiracy or collusion to commit acts of terrorism has been made a criminal offence so that prosecution of ephemeral terrorist networks is possible. In prosecuting offences of conspiracy, "statements made by those who made the agreement" or "witness statements or tapped telephone conversations" can be used in a court of law.[12] The *Intelligence and Security Services Act 2002* permits AIVD to pass relevant information for investigations and prosecution to federal and regional police, military and judicial authorities and also to receive relevant information from those agencies to assist in security operations.[13]

With regard to domestic maritime security, the Dutch Navy is very much in a supporting role. The most recent Defence White Paper of 2000 outlines one of the future roles of the Dutch military as assisting the civilian authorities in the context of law enforcement, disaster relief and humanitarian aid, both nationally and internationally.[14] The Dutch naval forces incorporate both defence and security tasks in their domestic mandate requiring close cooperation with civilian departments. In fact, the Netherlands Coast Guard, which is part of the navy and has been under its operational control since 1995, is a cooperative framework comprising various central government departments. The Coast Guard Centre is manned by naval personnel and includes several liaison offices of other ministries involved.

Counter-terrorism is directed outside of the organization and is supported through the law enforcement portion of the Coast Guard mandate. However, the 7 Netherlands Special Boat Squadron, one of the Dutch Special Forces and Counter-Terrorism units which resides in the Royal Netherlands Marine Corps (which is in the navy), has British SAS-trained maritime special forces experts which are capable of counter-terrorism operations to protect offshore oil platforms from terrorist attack.[15]

Maritime security becomes a much more dominant concern for the Dutch as one enters inland waters and port facilities. A unique feature of maritime security in the Netherlands is the requirement to protect the numerous dykes that hold back the North Sea waters. This feature will not, however, be pursued in this study due to its singular application to the Netherlands. As in other countries since September 11, awareness of the vulnerabilities of commercial ports and shipping has increased. The United States has been a major driving force in raising awareness and reducing vulnerability. The EU adopted the International Marine Organization's International Ship and Port Facility Security (ISPS) Code as an EU Security Directive and the Netherlands, with so much invested in its major ports, has been a strong proponent of the US Customs Service's Container Security Initiative (CSI). A Dutch initiative is research in critical infrastructure and computer network protection. Recovery times and impact levels have been calculated in order to inform policy-makers which priorities to focus on in the event of a catastrophic attack.

Prioritizing Approaches to Maritime Security

The Netherlands has engaged various facets of national power using traditional departmental and interdepartmental solutions to ensure that limited resources are used prudently to answer the maritime security challenge. In doing so, the Dutch have developed a method of prioritization that fills vulnerability gaps according to their importance. As have other countries in the West, the Netherlands has had to embark on both strategic and tactical responses to improve the security of ships, ports, territorial and coastal waterways, offshore exploitation activities, international waters, and national interests in foreign waters and ports.

Once again, collaboration, domain awareness, safeguarding and responsiveness will be utilized as key factors to illustrate how the Netherlands prioritizes its security activities. The government's use of resource allocation, changes to machinery of government, amendments to legislation, policy development, information sharing, changes to intelligence organization mandates, and the establishment of warning and assessment capability will serve as indicators of priority in the Dutch maritime security process.

Collaboration
The complexity of access and usage demands on the Netherlands North Sea has generated an impressive strategic governance and management structure that interlocks international, national and regional debate and policy development. Of the four key factors, the Dutch make collaboration their highest priority.[16] Many issues such as boundaries, fishing quotas and shipping routes are determined by international organizations and are beyond the Dutch government's control. However, over the last 25 years, institutions such as International Deliberations over North Sea Governance (IDON) and its predecessor the Interdepartmental Coordinating Committee for North Sea Affairs (ICONA) have debated, coordinated and formulated policies, directives and legislation

between ministries at the national level. It is this sort of organization that houses the national expertise requisite for composing national strategy and legislation.

When juggling conflicting strategic and political issues such as environment, economy, security and society, and there is a requirement for a maritime focus, the Dutch government is well served by a body that can "debate policies, management strategies, laws, permits and other similar instruments at regular intervals at international, ministerial, and operational levels to achieve an integrated system of cooperative governance."[17] The Netherlands has succeeded in this collaborative effort at the strategic level by ensuring an organization of great breadth that is not a cabinet committee (which means that it is removed from political exigencies and can focus on maritime security in the long term), has the tools to find compromise in national policy-making, and has the linkages to assert Dutch strategic interests in wider forums.

The second collaborative approach is legislation in the Netherlands regarding the Dutch secret service. The *Intelligence and Security Services Act 2002* and the *Crimes of Terrorism Act 2004* open a new chapter in the Dutch government's ability to prosecute terrorists and their supporters. The General Intelligence and Security Service (AIVD) is given its duties and powers in the *Intelligence and Security Services Act 2002*. Of particular note are the articles pertaining to cooperation with the various levels of police, the National Public Prosecutor and the Royal Netherlands Military Constabulary. AIVD is directed to support these agencies by furnishing information and providing technical support whenever possible.[18] The implicit link that the Regional Intelligence Services of the police forms between AIVD and the Dutch Police augments the value to national security through "the "antenna function" of the police forces in the regional and local communities."[19]

The *Crimes of Terrorism Act 2004* sets out the legal nature of recruiting for terrorist organizations and conspiracy to commit a terrorist act, and the ability to utilize AIVD documents in a court of law. There has been some controversy about this legislation. Many Dutch legal scholars believe that it is foreign to Dutch law to make conspiracy punishable—i.e., to punish for *a motive* rather than *an act*. They argue that from there "it is a small step to make criminal thoughts punishable."[20]

Safeguarding

A close second in priority for maritime security is safeguarding. The foundation of safeguarding is the ISPS Code and the various security upgrades that it directs member countries to adopt. Following on from the ISPS Code, the Netherlands was the first country outside the United States to embrace the US Customs approach named the Container Security Initiative (CSI). There are four main elements of CSI:

- standard criteria for high-risk containers;
- developing pre-screening technology;
- a pre-screening process prior to arrival in port; and
- the use of "smart" containers.

Of the eight EU countries that signed bilateral agreements with the United States, the Netherlands was the first to invite US Customs officers into its ports to commence CSI training on 26 August 2002. These teams pre-screen high-risk containers for weapons of mass destruction using "radiological portal monitors" at Rotterdam.[21] By coordinating intelligence and transport information with pre-screening capability, it is possible to minimize the risk from the handling of over three million containers each year.

An additional safeguard, focused specifically at the huge port of Rotterdam, is the federally-run Rotterdam-Rijnmond Seaport Police force or *Zeehavenpolitie*. This special police force is responsible for environmental enforcement, shipping safety, port safety and security, and combating terrorism and organized crime within the harbour limits.[22] It is a modern, fully-equipped force with 13 vessels and 40 patrol vehicles. Its key tasks are border control and security.

Responsiveness
In the maritime approaches and in ports, it would be the Dutch police, assisted by Coast Guard coordination, that would take responsibility for responding to terrorist threats and enforcing the law. Any arrest would take place inside the 12-mile territorial limit where national laws apply and would be performed by police forces supported by Coast Guard or naval vessels.

A particular Dutch strength in responsiveness is in the area of elite special forces units that are housed in Dutch military and law enforcement agencies. In the Royal Netherlands Marine Corps, the 7 Netherlands Special Boat Squadron has been trained specifically by the renowned British special forces to bolster security in maritime venues. The members of this unit are skilled parachutists, scuba divers and demolition experts. The unit is specifically trained in maritime counter-terrorism operations. It is broken into several sub-units: a boating unit; an underwater unit; an insertion unit which uses underwater vehicles and small craft; and an anti-terrorist group. With a complement of 23 men and two officers, it takes responsibility for responding to threats to Dutch passenger liners, ferries and particularly Dutch offshore oil platforms from terrorist attack.[23] The stealth, mobility and strength of these special forces make them ideal assets for responding to terrorist threats to maritime facilities and vehicles.

Domain Awareness
Due to the high density and complexity of the vessel traffic flow off the coast of the Netherlands and the international organization for managing traffic, the Dutch give a lower priority than our other case-countries to domain awareness outside their territorial

waters. Of the four key factors, it rates last in priority.[24] Once the vessel traffic enters Dutch territorial waters and internal traffic systems, the focus on individual ship information increases. In any case, the focus of domain awareness is on safety and pollution control through the coordinated effort of six departments led by the Coast Guard.

While compromises have been made in maritime surveillance, the Dutch approach to foreign intelligence is robust and cooperative in nature. Since the abolishment of the Foreign Secret Service in 1994, the foreign signals intelligence capability held in the Technical Information Processing Centre (TIVC) in Amsterdam is under the control of the Military Intelligence Service. However, the broad approach that evolved to confront international terrorism in the *Intelligence and Security Services Act 2002* allows the AIVD to access the information held in the TIVC and to conduct intelligence activities in other countries to investigate phenomena such as terrorism, illegal migration, and other non-military activities. The prevention of terrorist acts by targeted intelligence clearly has the preference.

Beyond the coalitions related to the UK, USA, NATO, and bilateral arrangements, the Netherlands is an active participant in a number of intra-European groups.[25] This propensity to join into the larger international effort confirms that the government "supports the vision that international terrorism can only be fought with an international coalition."[26]

Conclusion

The approaches that the Dutch government has adopted to enhance maritime security stem from the compromises that the Netherlands has had to make given its strong support of multilateral institutions and its key strategic position as a trade hub for an enlarged Europe. As such, the Dutch must often abide by decisions (or the lack of decisions) and compromises that are made by the larger community. With limitations on flexibility due to the constraints from community memberships, the Netherlands has opted to gain the maximum utility from relationships between countries, departments and agencies at the various levels of Dutch government and society.

In maritime security, the Dutch rank collaboration first, safeguarding second, domain awareness third and responsiveness fourth.[27] The placement of safeguarding after collaboration is due to the complex, interdependent strategic situation in which the Netherlands finds itself (which makes physical domain awareness less achievable) and the high value placed on infrastructure of hub-ports and maritime assets which factor so strongly in the Dutch economy. Compared to other countries' approaches, which stem from different strategic priorities, several of these approaches rise above the others as best practices that can be considered particularly useful for governments wishing to improve their maritime security policy in the altered threat environment.

Notes

1. *The World Factbook 2004*, Netherlands.
2. Energy Information Administration, "North Sea Regional Country Analysis Brief," Energy Information Administration website (August 2004). Available from http://www.eia.doe.gov/emeu/cabs/northsea.html (Cited 16 September 2004).
3. "Netherlands Background Notes."
4. *Ibid.*
5. North Atlantic Treaty Organization, "Prague Summit: Adapting to the Threat of Terrorism," North Atlantic Treaty Organization website (22 June 2004). Available from http://www.nato.int/terrorism/index.htm (Cited 16 September

2004).
6. Stevenson, "How Europe and America Defend Themselves," p. 83.
7. *Ibid.*
8. Kevin O'Brien, Erik van de Linde, et al., "Quick Scan of post 9/11 National Counter-terrorism Policymaking and Implementation in Selected European Countries." *Counter-terrorism in Europe*, RAND Organization website. Available from http://www.rand.org/randeurope/review/1.4-obrien.html (Cited 15 September 2004), p. 81.
9. Micheal Barry, Ina Elema and Paul van der Molen, "Ocean Governance in the Netherlands North Sea," in FIG (Federation Internationales des Geometres) *Working Week 2003* (Paris, 2003), p. 13. Available from http://www.fig.net/pub/fig_2003/TS_20/TS20_2_Barry_et_al.pdf (Cited 16 September 2004).
10. Eric Akerboom, "Counter-terrorism in the Netherlands," Federation of American Scientists website (October 2003), p. 8. Available from http://www.fas.org/irp/world/netherlands/ct.pdf (Cited 16 September 2004).
11. Netherlands, Department of Justice, "Dutch Senate Agrees to Crimes of Terrorism Act," Netherlands Justice website (21 June 2004). Available from http://www.justitie.nl/english/press/press_releases/archive/ archive_2004/240604dutch_senate_agrees_to_crimes_of_terrorism_act.asp (Cited 16 September 2004).
12. *Ibid.*
13. Jelle van Buuren, "Country Report – Netherlands," The Association for Progressive Communications website (2001). Available from http://europe.rights.apc.org/c_rpt/netherlands.html (Cited 16 September 2004).
14. Netherlands, Ministry of Defence, *Defence White Paper 2000* (Netherlands: Ministry of Defence, 1999), p. 2.
15. Dominique Sumner, "Dutch Special Forces and Counter

Terrorist Units," Special Forces website. Available from http:/
/www.specwarnet.net/europe/dutch_overview.htm (Cited 16
September 2004), p. 1.

16. Captain (N) Dick Ooms, Director Command, Control, Communications, Computers and Intelligence (C4I), Netherlands
Ministry of Defence Headquarters, phone interview by author, Ottawa/Amsterdam, 5 August 2004.

17. Barry, Elema and van der Molen, "Ocean Governance in the
Netherlands North Sea," p. 13.

18. Akerboom, "Counter-terrorism in the Netherlands," p. 3.

19. *Ibid.*, p. 4.

20. International Helsinki Federation, "The Netherlands IHF Focus," International Helsinki Federation website (July 2004).
Available from http://www.ihf-hr.org/viewbinary/
viewdocument.php?download=1&doc_id=5530 (Cited 16
September 2004), p. 3.

21. Sean Holstege, "Port Security a Rising Global Concern," *Tri-
Valley Herald* website (May 2004). Available from http://
www.trivalleyherald.com/Stories/
0,1413,86%257E10669%257E1622334,00.html (Cited 16
September 2004).

22. Senate of Canada, "Canada's Coastlines: The Longest Un-
der-Defended Borders in the World," *Report of the Standing
Senate Committee on National Security and Defence*, 37th
Parliament, 2nd Session, Vol. II, October 2003, p. 31.

23. Sumner, "Dutch Special Forces and Counter Terrorist Units,"
p. 3.

24. Captain (N) Dick Ooms, interview.

25. Rudner, "Hunters and Gatherers," p. 210.

26. O'Brien, van de Linde, et al., "Quick Scan of post 9/11 National Counter-terrorism Policymaking and Implementation
in Selected European Countries," p. 79.

27. Captain (N) Dick Ooms, interview.

CHAPTER 5
CASE STUDY, NORWAY

Overview: Maritime Perspective

Norway is bordered by Russia, Finland and Sweden to the east but its longest border is with three seas—the North, the Norwegian and the Barents, to the south, west and north. Straddling the Arctic Circle, it is the most northerly country in Europe and while it is Europe's fifth largest country by surface area, its population is only 4.5 million people.[1] Norway's rugged coastline is 21,925 kilometres long and thus its Economic Exclusion Zone (EEZ) is very large.[2] The coast is deeply indented with steep-sloped fjords and the northern third is topped by glaciers. The majority of its population centres are ports that are most often found protected from the sea inside the fjords. Oslo, the capital city, is one of the largest of the world's trading sea ports.

Norway has a strong economy, and as noted earlier boasts a high per capita GDP.[3] It is the world's third largest shipping state in terms of tonnage owned.[4] Norway owns the majority of the 714 ships of the Norwegian Merchant Marine that are over 1,000 tons, a huge accomplishment for a country with such a modest population. The Norwegian government observes that the terrorist threat against its fleet would likely occur outside Norway mainly because "the Norwegian fleet is engaged in crosstrades, and rarely calls at Norwegian ports."[5] Security measures taken in foreign ports would definitely have a marked effect on interaction with Norwegian ships in the future. Consequently, Norway recognizes the importance of working with the United States and the International Marine Organization (IMO) in pursuit of global maritime security. Maritime traffic along the Norwegian coast is constant, combining local traffic between ports, fishing traffic, tourist liners and merchant traffic.

Close to 70% of Norwegian exports relate to maritime activity—Norway has been the world's third largest oil exporter for several years producing about 4.3% of the world's oil, and it is an important exporter of fish and fish products.[6] The North Sea is spotted predominantly with Norwegian and English offshore oil platforms—an indicator of Norway's recent economic success in this sector. The offshore oil fields also have strategic importance in that "Norway may adjust its output in coordination with OPEC production increases and decreases" thereby playing an important role in the adjustment of world oil prices when demand fluctuates.[7] However, some of the older North Sea oil fields are in decline so natural gas has recently become a focus for exploitation. Norway, along with the Netherlands, is now a key European supplier of natural gas from new fields that have come on line not just in the North Sea but in the Norwegian Sea and Barents Sea as well. A constant tension between environmental concerns and petroleum exploitation keeps the Norwegian government balancing its future options.

The rich ecosystems of the marine and coastal areas, particularly in the northerly Barents Sea, are another resource that Norway wants to nurture and from which it wants to benefit. It is the desire for special care in the management of these resources which has prompted Norway to start negotiations for the increase of its territorial waters zone from four nautical miles to the usual 12 nautical miles.

A constitutional monarchy with a parliamentary system, Norway has a strong and open democracy that encourages cooperation with the rest of the international community. While it is a strong supporter of multilateral institutions like the United

Nations and NATO, Norway chose to remain out of the European Union in both 1972 and 1994. It is not represented in the European Commission, the Council of the EU, or the European Parliament. The krone remains Norway's currency and its monetary policy is aimed at maintaining stability against the euro. It must be noted, however, that Norway is part of the EU Internal Market through its membership in the Agreement on the European Economic Area. This extends the internal market (except the agricultural and fisheries sectors) and its free movement of goods, capital, services and persons to Norway. Moreover, due to this agreement Norway is consulted on proposals for European legislation once they have been presented to the Council of the EU.

Due to its petroleum-rich economy, Norway achieves a certain independence and flexibility to which other members of the EU cannot aspire. While Norway remains closely tied to its main economic partner (the EU), it has been able to continue with independent legislation that caters specifically to Norwegian interests and values without being forced into the compromises required of the larger community.

Norway has an immigrant population of 333,000 persons which accounts for 7.3 per cent of the total population. Seventy per cent of the immigrant population originates from non-Western countries—the largest sources being Pakistan, Iraq, Somalia, Morocco and Bosnia-Herzegovina.[8] Thirty-seven per cent live in Oslo, Norway's capital and largest port. The Norwegian government has recognized that Norway will likely become a "multicultural" society and has commissioned a report which was presented to Parliament in the fall of 2004. In view of current statistics which display a certain unease with immigrant society, the government has commenced a number of innovative initiatives, such as public readings in municipal libraries between mixed audiences to assist in the integration process.[9]

Norway does not as of yet have deep concerns about the possibility of terrorism inside the country. After 9/11, a Norwegian poll indicated that 60 per cent of Norwegians were not worried about the terrorism threat.[10] The government is working hard to alleviate what concerns there are about immigrants and terrorism by promoting multiculturalism and eliminating racism amongst its citizens. Only recently (2004) have Norwegians started to feel that it is possible that terrorists could choose Norway as a place to live.[11]

National Security Developments

Norway is not part of the EU's Common Foreign and Security Policy nor is it part of the EU's Common Security and Defence Policy. However, Norway has regular political dialogues with the EU on foreign policy issues and is regularly invited to align itself with EU foreign policy statements. Furthermore, Norway has been invited to contribute to the military capabilities of the EU Rapid Reaction Force and to take part in the EU Police Mission that carries out crisis management in Bosnia.[12]

From the military perspective, as in other countries in the post-9/11 world, Norwegian security depends on forces that can adapt to the diversity and unpredictability of modern threats through agility and technological superiority. The government has decided to continue its custom of conscription for one year's service.[13] The Norwegian Defence Minister is following the NATO lead in "transforming" Norway's military forces into smaller, better-equipped and better-prepared forces within a framework of close civil-military and allied cooperation. According to the Minister of Defence, Kristen Krohn Devold, "Transformation means re-shaping the military body to give it the necessary agility, punch, technique and mobility to be usable in present and future security scenarios."[14] It is believed that the most efficient defence of Norway will begin in distant countries and that a traditional national territorial defence is unnecessary.

The Norwegian Navy is small and fast. Its small number of frigates and submarines are suited for both littoral and blue water; however, it is the 20 agile and stealthy fast patrol boats (a mixture of 14 old and six futuristic and very fast boats) that represents the strength of the Norwegian Navy in territorial and littoral waters. These versatile vessels can be utilized anywhere in the world in littoral waters.

The structure of the navy matches the spectrum of risks in the post-9/11 world and, as such, can fully contribute to Norway's security policy aims which are:

1. to prevent war and to contribute to stability and peaceful development;
2. to safeguard the rights and interests of Norwegians and to preserve Norway's freedom of action in the face of political and military duress; and
3. to safeguard Norwegian sovereignty.[15]

The Norwegian Coast Guard, which is a direct subordinate of the navy, has several principal tasks which include acting in support of Norwegian sovereignty, exercising authority in connection with fisheries and offshore resources, environmental monitoring, search and rescue coordination, and assisting other government departments and civil authorities.[16] These duties entail maintaining an appropriate presence in the large Norwegian EEZ, protecting fisheries around the mainland and around Svalbard and Jan Mayan, its islands to the north. Coast Guard officers can legally board and inspect any vessel in Norwegian waters, they can make arrests and seize vessels and, if denied access to a vessel, they can use power to board it forcibly. Their vessels are armed but the personnel usually are not. The Coast Guard has a number of capable patrol vessels and cutters, as well as a new ice-breaking surveillance vessel, to carry out these tasks. It leases up to seven civilian vessels for surveillance and fisheries patrol and seven vessels for inland pollution control. It also utilizes its six Lynx helicopters from shore bases as well as flying time from the navy's maritime patrol aircraft for surveillance. Furthermore, it leases civilian aircraft to augment observation and surveillance coverage.

Norway's military also includes a Home Guard which is composed of 600 peacetime members and can be mobilized to 83,000 members in times of crisis.[17] It consists of a Naval Home Guard and one for Land and Air. The potential to add ready, trained mariners who can execute safeguarding and reaction tasks to support the military in times of duress is an excellent asset.

Norway updated its anti-terrorism legislation in June 2002 with a bill entitled Legislative Measures Against Acts of Terrorism and the Financing of Terrorism.[18] The Norwegian Penal Code now makes it a serious criminal offence to commit or to finance terrorist acts directly or indirectly. The legislation also attaches criminal liability to acts committed to facilitate terrorist acts and indirectly prohibits recruitment to terrorist groups.[19] These laws follow the requirements of the UN International Convention for the Suppression of the Financing of Terrorism and the EU's Common Position on the application of specific measures to combat terrorism. Since the passing of this law, there have been few prosecutions. As of September 2003, Norway had not discovered any evidence that terrorist funds have been deposited in the country.[20]

Foreign intelligence in Norway has historical Cold War ties that presented an excellent foundation for intelligence cooperation and sharing in the post-9/11 era. For domestic security intelligence, the National Police Security Service (PST) under the Ministry of Justice and Police concerns itself with internal challenges to Norwegian law. However, the uncovering of sustained illegal surveillance activities by this agency in 1994 led to a judicial inquiry into the activities of the PST. The findings of the commission were "crushing" in their criticism of the secret service surveillance activities. This has resulted in great pressure and oversight reform of the service.[21]

The area of domestic security intelligence has been very delicate in the period of the war on terrorism. While most Norwegians do not feel overtly threatened by terrorism on their own soil, there are fears of terrorists hiding among asylum seekers.[22] Sharing this concern, the United States doubted the capacity of the Norwegian police to access information about terrorists from the resident Muslim communities.[23] Consequently, this led to American CIA personnel penetrating Muslim organizations in Norway, monitoring their activities, and investigating suspicious individuals without any control on the part of the Norwegian government and limited accountability to the National Police Security Service.[24] This caused a strong negative reaction in certain government agencies due to the unprecedented intervention into a sovereign state's national security affairs.[25]

The 2004 Mullah Krekar case in which all charges were dropped against a suspected terrorist leader has European and Norwegian justice experts engaged in heated debate.[26] Differences between American, Dutch and Norwegian laws concerning evidence and extradition have led to the freeing of a man who many believe is the head of one of the main subordinate groups to Al Qaida. The Norwegian inability to use evidence supplied by intelligence agencies shows the difficulty of prosecution in cases where there is an international context to the terrorist crime. Neither prosecution in Norway nor extradition to Jordan or Iraq was possible under the present Norwegian Penal Code interpretation.[27]

Prioritizing Approaches to Maritime Security

Utilizing the strength of its economy, the understanding of its geographical position as a maritime state, and the reassurance of multilateral ties, Norway has formed a maritime security apparatus that is particular to its needs. Its inherent flexibility due to its peripheral connection to the EU and its low level of concern about terrorist aggression against Norwegian soil has led Norway to adopt a legislative and physical stance that protects its economic future and its freedom to take unilateral decisions through law enforcement and civil-military cooperation. In order to ensure the security of its numerous ships, ports, waterways and offshore platforms, and Norwegian interests in foreign waters and ports, Norway has prioritized its approaches at the strategic and tactical levels.

Norway has chosen to order its maritime security approaches to match its perception of the threat. The government's close relationship to NATO and perception of the threat has caused small changes to resource allocation, legislation, policy development and information sharing that will serve as indicators of priority in the Norwegian maritime security process. In order to protect what they already have, the Norwegians have placed responsiveness at the forefront of maritime security priorities.

Responsiveness
Working in close cooperation with NATO to promote collective defence and civil-military cooperation to meet the challenges of new threats, Norway has for the most part maintained traditional machinery of government in the post-9/11 era. The main priority in maritime security has been placed on responsiveness so the authorities can react to threats both far from home and in home waters and ports. The elite police response unit called "Delta" responds to cases all across Norway from its base in the capital, Oslo. Combined with Delta, the police have 700 specially trained officers in regional response units at continuous high alert who can engage in counter-terrorist tactics on land, at sea, in ports, and particularly on offshore oil platforms.[28] After 9/11, Norway also activated and now maintains the police reserves for training in the event that they would be needed to supplement the regular

police counter-terrorist forces. Moreover, the military has the Armed Forces Special Command, known as the FSK, which is made up of "highly trained operatives specially selected from other Norwegian special forces units."[29] Through decisions at the political level, the FSK can be deployed to assist police in domestic counter-terrorist operations. These world-class commandos train intensely on aircraft, trains, passengers ships and very frequently on oil rigs in order to face threats to Norwegian interests. They have also been deployed overseas to Afghanistan to combat Al Qaida during *Operation Enduring Freedom.*[30]

Of note is the small size and agility of the Norwegian Navy. The government invested in fast patrol boats and a small number of frigates for coastal fjord defence during the Cold War years. The Norwegian Defence Budget of 2004, while downsizing personnel and selling property to release resources from operating costs, proposes to procure five new frigates and five new fast patrol boats as replacements for the aging navy.[31] This continuation of emphasis on "flexibility, operational availability, rapid response capability, and endurance" in vessels built for operations in the littoral areas not only fits NATO transformation requirements, it is completely suitable for coastal defence and security requirements when necessary to carry out civil-military operations for maritime security.[32]

Domain Awareness
Of the principal tasks given to the Norwegian Navy by the government "surveillance and control of inshore waters and the protection of Norwegian interests on the high seas" are listed first.[33] To realize this wide-ranging task, the navy, with the support of NATO, has put in place a radar surveillance system known as Coastal Radar Integration and Display System (CRIADS) to cover the northern half of Norway's coast. Funding for the southern half did not materialize from NATO so the Norwegian government is mustering national resources to blend less capable sys-

tems to the south into a national sensor network.[34] Recognizing the need for layered sensor capability that results in near-continuous coverage, Norway has upgraded its coastal chain of radars and integrated their output into CRIADS which will combine information from military sources, Vessel Traffic Systems, the IMO-required AIS system, radio direction finders, satellite information, aircraft radar surveillance information, and remote-controlled camera data.[35] The fusing of the information from these various sensors will achieve a 24/7 coverage and tracking of all vessels that enter Norwegian waters.

Safeguarding
While Norway has been one of the world's top supporters of the IMO's ISPS Code which entered into service on 1 July 2004, it is not the Norwegian approach to ISPS that draws attention for the activity of safeguarding. Safeguarding of Norwegian territory is helped by the military system Norway maintains. Due to its small size, Norway still engages in conscription. The training requirement for the Home Guard takes the first four months of the conscription period.[36] The Naval Home Guard consists of 5,760 officers and men. It is divided into 31 Naval Areas and boasts 31 boarding security teams.[37] These boarding security teams have ample legal authority to search and detain suspect vessels, but they do not have authority to arrest people. They must call for support from the Coast Guard in such cases.[38] Their main tasks are to carry out surveillance of their naval area, to guard designated points with access to seaward, and to provide support to the armed forces. This force, once mobilized, can bring 300 small vessels, 120 high-speed craft, and 120 coastal reporting stations to the table for maritime security operations.[39]

Collaboration
Due to its particular stance regarding defence and security, Norway has chosen to remain constant in government structure and

separate in lines of responsibility. However, its collaboration with NATO countries in defence and bilateral arrangements for international intelligence and police cooperation is evident. Norway's approach to collaboration in intelligence sharing is noteworthy. Its partners include the Nordic countries which share the same area of interest, bilateral arrangements with NATO allies, and most importantly arrangements with the United States, the UK and Germany.[40] Of particular importance is the NORUSA II agreement that has provided an invaluable intelligence link to the United States for decades.[41]

Terrorism is seen as a threat to Europe by Norwegians and therefore they work with Europol, the Financial Action Task Force (FATF) and the Egmont Group as well as the EU "Counter-Terrorism Group" and the longstanding Kilowatt Group (focused on Arab terrorism) to make a collaborative European team.[42] A special bilateral relationship that takes on heightened importance in the post-9/11 era is Norway's close rapport with Israel. For decades, the two countries have shared information and training possibilities. Norway has ratified all 12 of the international conventions and protocols relating to terrorism.

Conclusion

The importance that Norway has placed on its military and administrative ties with the NATO alliance has in some ways given it flexibility to stay independent in its selected approaches to maritime security, just as its decision to remain separate from the EU gives it political freedom and its petroleum resources give it economic freedom. Thus, its second national security aim, "to safeguard Norwegians' rights and interests and to preserve Norway's freedom of action in the face of political and military duress"[43] stands above protecting sovereignty in a military way and leads to a different set of priorities in its security approaches. Norway does not keep a large military force to protect its sovereignty; it depends on NATO to do the heavy lifting. This very important strategic decision allows Norway to apply scarce resources to security and the diplomatic means of protecting Norwegians' rights and their government's freedom to choose independently on the periphery of the EU. The economy and environment (which are linked to future economic strength) factor strongly in security concerns.

Terrorism is seen as a crime and a threat that is real, but it is a threat primarily directed at other states and foreign ports. The immigrant population is small and the government is progressive in facing the challenges of its integration into Norwegian society.

In maritime security, the Norwegians ranked responsiveness first, domain awareness second, safeguarding third, and collaboration last.[44] Norway prioritizes its national ability to respond with strength and agility to modern threats as the most important national security activity. To be able to respond in a timely and accurate fashion, domain awareness is critical and is thus placed second in importance. Furthermore, broad intelligence ties, mostly bilateral, potentially increase domain awareness. Due to the government's decision to retain conscription, Norway has a unique safeguarding capability in the Home Guard which is spread strategically across the country and trained to react when a threat requires it. Finally, while collaboration in intelligence sharing is excellent, overall collaboration is not a priority given the country's reliance on its national reactive strength.

Notes

1. The EEZ is a zone 200 nautical miles out from the coast. *The World Factbook 2004,* Norway.
2. *Ibid.*
3. The figure for 2003 is 33,000. *Ibid.*

4. Norway, Department of Defence, "Norwegian Defence Facts and Figures 2003," Department of Defence website (July 2004). Available from http://odin.dep.no/fd/engelsk/publ/ veiledninger/010011-120046/hov005-bn.html#hov.ing.6 (Cited 16 September 2004).
5. Oluf Ulseth, Norwegian State Secretary, "New Demands on the Shipping Industry – Maritime Security," ODIN Norway government website (12 September 2002). Available from http://www.odin.dep.no/nhd/engelsk/aktuelt/taler/taler_ politisk_ledelse/024001-090039/ (Cited 16 September 2004).
6. Energy Information Administration, "North Sea Regional Country Analysis Brief," Energy Information Administration website (August 2004). Available from http:// www.eia.doe.gov/emeu/cabs/northsea.html (Cited 16 September 2004).
7. *Ibid.*
8. Norway, "Statistics Norway: Immigration and Immigrants 2003," p. 1.
9. International Federation of Library Associations and Institutions, "Multicultural Populations," International Federation of Library Associations and Institutions website (April 2004). Available from http://www.ifla.org/VII/s32/news/no1.htm (Cited 16 September 2004).
10. "47 Percent Support US Bombing," *Aftenposten* website (11 October 2001). Available from http://www.aftenposten.no/ english/local/article210526.ece (Cited 16 September 2004).
11. Commander (Senior Grade) Trond Hermansen, Senior Staff Officer Sea in the Joint Communications Information Systems Staff at NATO NORTHCOM Headquarters in Stavanger, Norway, phone interview by author, Ottawa/Stavanger, 30 August 2004.
12. Norway and the EU's Common Foreign and Security Policy," *Norway – the Permanent Mission to the EU*. Brussels website (2003). Available from http://www.eu-norway.org/foreign/

Foreign+Policy.htm (Cited 16 September 2004).
13. Kristen Krohn Devold, Norwegian Minister of Defence, "The Norwegian Defence – Usability through Transformation" (speech originally delivered by Defence Minister Krohn Devold at the meeting of the Norwegian Atlantic Committee, Oslo, 2 February 2004). Available from http://www.atlanterhavskomiteen.no/publikasjoner/andre/i-tekster/20.htm (Cited 16 September 2004), p. 14.
14. *Ibid.*
15. Norway, Department of Defence, "Norwegian Defence Facts and Figures 2003," p. 1.
16. *Ibid.*, 3.
17. Norway, Department of Defence, "Norwegian Defence Facts and Figures 2003," p. 10.
18. US Department of State, "International Narcotics Combined Strategy Report 2003: Country Reports - Norway," US Department of State website (September 2003). Available from http://www.state.gov/g/inl/rls/nrcrpt/2003/vol2/html (Cited 16 September 2004).
19. *Ibid.*
20. *Ibid.*
21. "Surveillance by Secret Service more Extensive than Assumed," *The Norway Post*, 26 February 2002, p. 4.
22. "Fear of Terrorists Hiding Among Asylum Seekers," *The Norway Post*, 22 November 2003, p. 1.
23. Rudner, "Hunters and Gatherers," p. 215.
24. *Ibid.*
25. *Ibid.*
26. Statewatch, "All charges dropped against Krekar," Statewatch website (15 June 2004). Available from http://www.statewatch.org/news/2004/jun/12norway-krekar.htm (Cited 16 September 2004).
27. Statewatch, "Krekar case poses more questions than answers," *Statewatch Bulletin*, Vol. 13, No. 6 (November-December 2003), p. 1.

28. Frode Nordseth, "Norwegian Forces practicing Counter-terrorism," Norwegian Defence website (1 January 2003). Available from http://www.mil.no/languages/english/start/article. jhtml?articleID=36541 (Cited 16 September 2004), p. 2.

29. *Ibid.*

30. *Ibid.*, p. 3.

31. Norway, Department of Defence, "The Norwegian Defence Budget 2004," Norwegian Department of Defence website (8 October 2003). Available from http://odin.dep.no/fd/engelsk/aktuelt/pressem/010001-070028/dok-bn.html (Cited 16 September 2004).

32. Norway, Department of Defence, "Norwegian Defence Facts and Figures 2003," p. 5.

33. *Ibid.*

34. Commander Espen Sundal, former Operations Officer for NATO NORTHCOM Headquarters in Stavanger, Norway, phone interview by author, Ottawa/Stavanger, 19 August 2004.

35. NAVTEK, "NAVTEK VTMS/VTMIS Products," NAVTEK website (February 2004). Available from http://www.navtek.no/Sider/VTS_VTMIS.html (Cited 16 September 2004).

36. Norway, Department of Defence, "Norwegian Defence Facts and Figures 2003," p. 11.

37. *Ibid.*

38. Commander Espen Sundal interview.

39. *Ibid.*

40. Olav Riste, "'The Missing Dimension': The Diplomatic History of Intelligence," in Jenssen and Riste (eds), *Intelligence in the Cold War* (Oslo: NIDS, 2001), p. 136.

41. *Ibid.*, p. 139.

42. Rudner, "Hunters and Gatherers," pp. 210-211.

43. Norway, Department of Defence, "Norwegian Defence Facts and Figures 2003," p. 5.

44. Commander Espen Sundal interview.

CHAPTER 6
BEST PRACTICES

Setting the Stage

The three case-countries discussed here have displayed varying approaches to maritime security based on their individual perceptions of the threat and their national interests. Australia, a country with traditional concerns about illegal migration and regional unrest—as well as a verifiable Al Qaida attack on its citizens in Bali—has chosen a highly collaborative maritime security regime that depends primarily on domain awareness to alert authorities early so preventive action can be taken. The Netherlands also has concerns about its immigrant population but it is the multicultural trading hub for the new Europe. It sees its strength through international cooperation, and has also chosen to favour collaboration above all. The Netherlands, however, has stressed safeguarding next to ensure that its national interests are guarded in view of potential external and internal threats. Norway, which prizes its autonomy and seeks to protect its wealth in natural resources, overtly depends on alliances for defence concerns allowing it to concentrate on responsiveness and domain awareness to protect its national interests. The ability to protect sovereignty through military force has been dismissed by Norwegian decision-makers—they depend on NATO to do this. In so doing, resources focusing on security activities like responsiveness (highly trained police forces) and domain awareness (radar chains and surveillance emphasis) take the fore in mitigating and preventing the new threats that menace Norway.

As pointed out in Chapter 1, Canada, always conscious of its interdependence with the world's superpower, would seem to fit between the Netherlands and Australia favouring a collaborative approach and investing in domain awareness to meet a moderate concern about the modern threat situation.

Criteria for Best Practices

From the security approaches that have been described in the three case studies, and which are listed in Table 2, it is possible to select best practices with the aim of finding ideas to improve existing maritime security policy. In *Benchmarking for Best Practices in the Public Sector*, the authors make a special aim of defining and addressing the criteria for "best practices" in government and the public sector. As noted earlier, a "best practice" can be defined broadly as "anything better than your current practice."[1] However, while this general definition has some merit in that it highlights the relativity to the user's needs, the authors point out that it is too broad to be useful in selecting the top performing approaches among a group of approaches. A best practice blends together the ideas of mission success and steady improvement of procedures and practices over time.

Therefore, a best practice cannot just be a good idea, but it must be a proven, good idea in practice for a period that is worthy of assessment. For most government-related practices, a period of two to three years would be a minimum period for this criterion given the time required to carry out audit analysis during budget-cycle periods. In private business, the period of assessment could be markedly shorter.

A best practice must have tangible results or at least a "recognized positive outcome" that can be observed through awards, media attention, or other positive indicators.[2] It may be difficult to assess the success of a specific practice, particularly a preventative effort. It may be difficult to obtain indicators even if the project is successful due to classification restrictions. However, the practice may have a positive impact on some more common-place activities that are related to the security event (illegal immigration, for instance). A surveillance or collaboration effort aimed at reducing illegal immigration by sea may have a clear parallel to similar efforts against terrorism from the sea. Therefore, a recognized positive outcome for illegal immigration would be acceptable as a positive indicator for counter-terrorism efforts. While we cannot always know whether a preventive policy is successful, there are often recognized indicators of success in linked policies and practices. The recognition of these indicators of success can provide the necessary criteria for recognized positive outcome when tangible evidence concerning the maritime security approach is not obtainable.

And finally, the best practice must have local importance to the organization that is searching for improvement. A practice that is completely foreign to the experience of the searching organization will fail this test. For instance, a policy enacting close cooperation with regional partners in ocean surveillance may not be useful for the security framework of a country like Slovakia. For this study, Canada will be used as the country searching for improvement and, thus, the best practice must have local importance to Canada.

The approach does not have to be identical for the importing organization; however, a best practice should have the ability to be adopted elsewhere and create client satisfaction.[3] For the purposes of this monograph, best practices are defined as processes or approaches which:

- are successful over time;
- display a recognized positive outcome; and
- have local importance to Canada, the home country of the author of this paper.

To be a best practice, an approach must fulfill the requirements of *all three* criteria.

Clearly, applying these criteria to the complete list of approaches in Table 2 will reduce the number of possible new ideas to improve security. Countries vary in their capabilities and access to resources, but all states must be able to provide security for themselves. However, due to the filtering for applicability to Canada, the three best practices criteria will assist in finding the optimum approaches that are applicable to the Canadian maritime security system. It is important to be aware, however, that best practices may not be importable even when all the criteria have been fulfilled. As noted in the case-country studies, the countries all have unique national security requirements, and what may work in one country may not work in another. As well, the importing country may not be ready right away to accept the practice in its national system. It is also important to realize that other methods to achieve an approach could exist elsewhere—the fact that an approach is excluded from this best practices list does not mean that the idea is a bad one, just that the particular form of the approach does not meet the requirements of this study.

Best Practice Criteria versus Maritime Security Approaches

By referring to Table 2, the reader can follow the comparison of best practice criteria to the 21 approaches taken from the three case studies. The comparison process will vet out approaches that do not fulfill criteria requirements. Those approaches that remain after this comparison will be chosen as the best practices of this study.

Starting with the criteria that the approach must be "successful over time," the following approaches fail to meet the criteria requirements:

#3   agreements with regional partners;

#7   funding to Customs department vice Port Authorities;

#8   financial aid to regional partners;

#9   legislation for ASIO's powers of detention;

#10 national alert system;

#12 legislation for cooperation between intelligence and law enforcement; and

#20 Naval Home Guard.

The majority of these approaches do not meet the "successful over time" criteria simply because, while they show promise, they have not been in existence long enough nor tested for success.

Table 2: Maritime Security Approaches and Best Practices (✓✓)

APPROACH	Successful over Time	Recognized Positive Outcome	Local Importance (Canada)
1. Whole-of-Government Approach (Aus)	✓✓	✓✓	✓✓
2. Common Risk Assessment (Aus)	✓✓	✓✓	✓✓
3. Agreements – Regional Partners (Aus)	?	?	?
4. Coastwatch – Civil-Air Emphasis (Aus)	✓✓	✓✓	✓✓
5. National Operations Centre (Aus)	✓	✓	?
6. ASIS (Foreign Intelligence Service) (Aus)	✓✓	✓✓	✓✓
7. Not funding Port Authorities (Aus)	?	?	?
8. Financial Aid to Regional Partners (Aus)	?	✓	?
9. ASIO – Powers of Detention (Aus)	?	?	✓
10. National Alert System (Aus)	?	✓	✓
11. IDON – Oceans Governance (Neth)	✓✓	✓✓	✓✓
12. Law - Law Enforcement/Intelligence (Neth)	?	✓	✓
13. Container Security Initiative Leader (Neth)	✓	✓	?
14. Federal Major Port Police (Zeehaven) (Neth)	✓✓	✓✓	✓✓
15. Special Forces – Maritime (Neth)	✓	✓	?
16. Foreign Intelligence Collaboration (Neth)	✓	✓	?
17. Elite Response Units – Police (Nor)	✓✓	✓✓	✓✓
18. Small, Agile Naval Ships (Nor)	✓	?	?
19. Surveillance Radar Chains (Nor)	✓	?	?
20. Naval Home Guard (Nor)	?	✓	?
21. Broad Bilateral Intelligence Sharing (Nor)	✓	✓	?

(At the time of writing this paper, 2001 was only two years in the past—and thus many of the approaches that have been cited were less than two years old and had not been audited or tested for success.) The exceptions to this are the national alert system which has received wide-spread criticism as well as lukewarm public response and the Naval Home Guard which has not been mobilized for a security event in the recent past.

While the criterion "recognized positive outcome" of certain approaches is at times difficult to measure due to their preventive nature, positive outcome can be observed through awards, media attention, or other positive indicators such as an indication of having a positive impact on a commonplace activity that is related to the security event. Public denouncement of an approach could be an indicator of failure in this area.

Recognition of success in a related activity (ability to detect and track fishing boats off coastal waters, for example) may be a positive indication of a similar capability needed for counter-terrorist efforts. Of the approaches listed in this study, recognized positive outcome is failed by the following approaches: #3 - agreements with regional partners; #7 - financial aid to Customs vice Port Authorities; #9 - legislation for ASIO's powers of detention; #18 - small, agile naval ships; and #19 - coastal surveillance chains. The reason for failure in these cases is predominantly a lack of measurable or even indicative positive outcome from the approach. While Norway's small and agile naval ships and coastal radar chains were seen to be positive in the Cold War versus Soviet threats in Norwegian territorial waters, there has been little outcome apparent against merchant shipping and possible terrorist/criminal threats.

Finally, the "local importance to Canada" criterion is perhaps more capable of discrimination because it requires not just a good idea, but an idea that Canada has not already put into action and one that is desirable or possible given Canada's national values and interests. The following approaches fail this criterion for the above reasons: #3 - agreements with regional partners; #5 - national operations centre; #7 - financial aid to Customs vice Port Authorities; #8 - financial aid to regional partners; Container Security Initiative; #15 - special forces for maritime counter-terrorism; #16 - foreign intelligence through collaboration; #18 - small, agile naval ships; #19 - coastal surveillance radar chains; #20 - Naval Home Guard; and #21 - wide bilateral intelligence sharing. In most cases failure is simply due to the fact that Canada either already has a very similar approach or has policy to advance development in that area. The Naval Home Guard is exceptional given that it is based on a national policy of conscription that is not likely for Canada's future. Financial aid to regional partners does not apply to Canada as its trade is dominated by the United States and regional partners are not significant

Table 3: Best Practices—Country and Key Activity

Best Practice – Approach	Country	Key Activity
1. Whole-of-Government Approach	Australia	Collaboration
2. Common Risk Assessment	Australia	Collaboration
3. Coastwatch – Civil-Air Emphasis	Australia	Domain Awareness
4. ASIS – Foreign Human Intelligence	Australia	Domain Awareness
5. IDON – Ocean Governance	Netherlands	Collaboration
6. Federal Port Police – Zeehaven	Netherlands	Safeguarding
7. Elite Response Units – Police	Norway	Responsiveness

ingress sources to Canada. Small, agile naval ships would be helpful to Canada for coastal surveillance and law enforcement; however, that gap has already been recognized in Canada and force structure plans are being debated to address it.[4]

The resulting list of best practices is displayed in Table 3. These approaches have been successful over time, have shown a recognized positive outcome, and have local importance to Canada. There are three best practices that are collaboration activities, two that are domain awareness activities, and one each for safeguarding and responsiveness.

Seven Maritime Security Best Practices

While there is no order of importance for the seven best practices, the most strategic approach of the group is the "whole-of-government approach" for collaboration. Due to circumstances that were unique to Australia (regional instability, concern over international organized crime, the 2000 Olympics, unwanted maritime migration, and the East Timor crisis), the government embarked on new directions in legislation, information sharing, security resource management and changes to organizational structure. By cultivating an expectation for departments to share information and coordinate action both horizontally inside federal and state governments and vertically among municipal, state and federal levels, the national security effort has achieved an integrated product which continues to improve on founding principles. The success of this approach was apparent in the above-mentioned events and also in the reaction to Bali and the war on terrorism as well as numerous anti-migration incidents in recent years.

Aspects of the "whole-of-government approach," especially concerning legislation, intelligence coordination with law enforcement and interdepartmental features of government, would address the concerns of the Canadian Senate with respect to linkages between the federal government and first responders.[5] The Australian model could be transportable with modifications to act as an example for Canadian national and maritime security organization.

The Common Risk Assessment Methodology is a tactical-level best practice for collaboration. A recommendation by the Australian National Audit Office, this approach laid the foundation for a common language amongst resource users such that they could compete for federally-managed resources in a fair manner that is acceptable to all members of the maritime security community. The methodology has been operational for two years and has enabled Customs Coastwatch to adjust the resource balance across the country according to intelligence assessments that have been agreed upon three months prior to the date of operations.[6] This has led to dramatic decreases in illegal migration due to the capability of placing the right resources in the right area at the right time. This process combines preventive information sharing with adroit resource management that could be adapted by Canadian federal and provincial agencies to assist resource management across the Atlantic, Pacific and Arctic coasts as well as the Great Lakes and other inland waterways.

The complex maritime security environment in which the Netherlands is located has spawned a powerful strategic best practice in the form of the International Deliberations over North Sea Governance (IDON). Free from the rigours of Cabinet time constraints, this permanent committee combines decision-makers from across all departments to debate maritime-related laws and policies in a decidedly complex environment in which political issues of economy, environment, security and society overlap. For 25 years this group has ensured that a unified and prepared Dutch voice is heard in national, EC/EU and international forums. The ongoing success in winning Dutch interpretations of water boundaries and traffic routing is an indicator of this committee's value.[7] Canada has an *Ocean's Act* which is evolving to integrate the many issues involved in maritime security. A Canadian version of IDON would ensure a unified Canadian voice to work on governance issues between states, particularly in the changing Arctic region of Canada.

The best practices in domain awareness are both focused on enriching the maritime picture in and around Australia. The emphasis on civil-air surveillance has allowed Customs Coastwatch to improve dramatically its understanding of what is happening in the maritime approaches, ports and foreign ports—the essence of domain awareness. Plans for future surveillance would incorporate satellite and UAV information with that of the current leased aircraft to further automate the process. Coastwatch has utilized civil-surveillance since 1987. Notable indicators of successful domain awareness stand out. Australia has been able to increase the number of apprehensions of illegal migrants from 42 in 1998/99 to 162 apprehensions in 2002/03.[8] Furthermore, illegal arrivals by sea plummeted from between three and four thousand *each year* between 1999 and 2001 to less than 10 in the years 2002 and 2003.[9] With 83 staff members, 17 aircraft flying 4,500 surveillance missions, and costs of $70 million (Australian dollars) for contracts each year, Coastwatch has succeeded in satisfying its clients and fulfilling its government mission for domain awareness.

While Canadian Departments of Fisheries and Defence have contracted Provincial Air Lines on both coasts in recent years to augment military surveillance flights, the scale is tiny and domain awareness is patchy at best.[10] And surveillance of the Arctic is even less. Civil air surveillance of this sort is an option that could improve Canada's maritime domain awareness to desired levels on all three coasts and in the interior—a government priority.[11]

The other side of domain awareness is intelligence which serves to populate the database of known information about vessels, personnel and cargo that appear in a country's area of interest. The Australian Secret Intelligence Service (ASIS) functions secretly in the interests of Australia's national security and interests under the Minister of Foreign Affairs. It uses human intelligence from foreign countries and through connections with other international partners to increase the domain awareness of the maritime security community. It was given this particular mandate through national legislation in 2001. Since then, it has been a valued member of all maritime security committees at all levels and has added a proactive, foreign perspective to domain awareness. In other words, ASIS does not just use its intelligence to advise policy-makers; it is an integral, participating part of the maritime and national security fabric by law.

While the Canadian Secret Intelligence Service (CSIS) has a small, and possibly growing, capability in human security intelligence outside Canada, there is no dedicated foreign espionage agency in Canada.[12] Furthermore, there is an ongoing debate in government circles over how such an agency should relate to the legislative act establishing and defining CSIS.[13] It has been stated by top Canadian government officials that Canada would be well-served by a foreign intelligence agency that could integrate into threat situations and share information freely with other states that also carry out foreign intelligence.[14] The ASIS model for foreign intelligence is transportable to Canada, but it is likely not compatible with the present CSIS arrangement.

The best practice for safeguarding is a specialized federal police force that is used specifically in a municipal jurisdiction of the major national port. Tasked with border enforcement and security within the harbour limits, the Rotterdam-Rijnmond Seaport Police share information and cooperate with federal intelligence and law enforcement agencies in order to take proactive security measures in the giant city of the world's largest port. This configuration has existed for 10 years. Recent arrests and prosecutions of terrorist suspects in Rotterdam attest to the deterrent and preventive value of this force. Moreover, the Australian government and officials from Brisbane have conducted liaison meetings to gain from the Seaport police experience.[15]

Through the 1990s, Canada privatized all ports. In recent years Canada has been criticized for lack of capability in port security.[16] While there have been efforts to include federal enforcement personnel in the major ports, Canada still does not have enough police presence and capability in many active ports.[17] The federally-run port police approach is worth considering for the 20 major ports that are crucial to trade and ferry traffic. There may also be value in such a force to watch over the various seaways and canal systems that are so important to Canada's maritime trade system.

While most of the case-countries placed priority on collaboration and domain awareness, only Norway chose responsiveness as its top key activity. As such, the widespread use of the elite police response units factors as a best practice in a more reactive activity area. The combination of the elite Delta response unit and specially-trained police officers in all regions provides the round-the-clock capability to carry out counter-terrorism tactics in all maritime venues across the country. Furthermore, the cross-training with the military special forces known as FSK ensures that tactical hand-offs to world-class operatives works smoothly in all counter-terrorism activities including vessel take-downs or oil platform assaults. While actual positive indicators for performance are not easy to cite, the top-notch training with other world leaders and recent success in the war on terrorism are indicators that the capability is strong and oriented directly toward maritime challenges, among others.

Canada has the Joint Task Force Two special force unit in its military which has a single, small maritime special force section. Law enforcement agencies do not have specific maritime counter-terrorism forces although the RCMP has armed ship boarding teams that can board and seize a vessel. The funding for these teams has been assessed as insufficient.[18] The cross-country training of port-city police forces in maritime counter-terrorism tactics, specialist police maritime counter-terrorism forces, and cooperative mandates with military special forces would markedly improve Canada's ability to react in an area that has been identified as weak.[19]

Notes

1. Patricia Keehley, et al., *Benchmarking for Best Practices in the Public Sector*, p. 19.
2. *Ibid.*, p. 26.
3. *Ibid.*, p. 24.
4. Senate of Canada, "Canada's Coastlines: The Longest Under-Defended Borders in the World," in *The Report of the Standing Committee on National Security and Defence*, p. 24. Vice-Admiral Ron Buck describes these craft and states that they are in the defence services program.
5. Senate of Canada, "National Emergencies: Canada's Fragile Frontlines," in *The Report of the Standing Committee on National Security and Defence*, 37th Parliament, 2nd Session, Vol. I (March 2004), Chapter 7.
6. "Overview of Customs Coastwatch," p. 5.
7. Barry, Elema and van der Molen, "Ocean Governance in the Netherlands North Sea," pp. 13-14.
8. Australia, Official Coastwatch Presentation to the Canadian Navy, Canberra: National Surveillance Centre, 25 February 2004.
9. *Ibid.*
10. Senate of Canada, "Canada's Coastlines: The Longest Under-Defended Borders in the World," pp. 20-21.
11. Canada, Department of Transport, *Enhancing the Security of Canada's Marine Transportation System*, p. 8.
12. Ward Elcock, Director, Canadian Security Intelligence Serv-

ice, "The John Tait Memorial Lecture" (presentation given
by Mr. Elcock to the CASIS Conference in Vancouver, BC,
17 October 2003). Available from http://www.csis-scrs.gc.ca/
eng/miscdocs/director20031017_e.html (Cited 17 September 2004).

13. Martin Rudner, "Contemporary Threats, Future Tasks: Canadian Intelligence and the Challenges of Global Security,"
in N. Hillmer and M.A. Molot (eds), *Canada Among Nations 2002: A Fading Power* (Don Mills, ON: Oxford University Press, 2002), p. 163.

14. David Pratt, "Foreign Intelligence in the New Security Environment," in David Rudd and David McDonough (eds), *Canadian Strategic Forecast 2004 – The 'New Security Environment': Is the Canadian Military up to the Challenge?* (Toronto: The Canadian Institute of Strategic Studies, 2004), p. 10.

15. "Rotterdam Seaport Police," *Netherlands Immigration Department* website (2004). Available from http://www.dutch-immigration.nl/uk_info_rivpol.htm (Cited 17 September 2004).

16. Senate of Canada, "Canadian Security and Military Preparedness," in *The Report of the Standing Committee on National Security and Defence*, 37th Parliament, 2nd Session (February, 2002), pp. 37-39.

17. Brian Daly, "Mounties want more money, staff for port security, says RCMP manager," Recorder.ca website (3 May 2004). Available from http://www.recorder.ca/cp/National/040502/n050217A.html (Cited 17 September 2004).

18. Senate of Canada, "Canada's Coastlines: The Longest Under-Defended Borders in the World," pp. 28-29.

19. *Ibid.*, p. 57. Recommendation 2.5 concerns the designation of the RCMP as the lead police force for all air and sea ports and adequate funding to combat security breaches.

CHAPTER 7
CONCLUSION

The seven best practices that were identified in Chapter 6 represent proven approaches to maritime security that have shown success over time through positive indications and have a local importance for Canada. Out of the many approaches to maritime security surveyed, these best practices stood in a class of their own according to the criteria that were selected. If one compiles the number of best practices by country, there are four from Australia, two from the Netherlands, and one from Norway. Table 4 assists the reader to visualize the overarching comparison.

The best practices from this study contain a mix of preventive and reactive approaches, although a solid majority are preventive in nature. There are three collaboration approaches, two domain awareness approaches, one safeguarding approach and one responsiveness approach.

It is evident that best practices have a relationship between national perception of threat and national response through maritime security activities. On the one hand, countries such as Australia that feel a threat directly, particularly that of strategic terrorism, are likely to heavily weigh their priorities in favour of cooperative and proactive approaches in the key activity areas of collaboration and domain awareness. By enacting these preventive approaches, the countries so disposed seek actively to prevent major attacks on native soil and to neutralize the threat before it takes shape far beyond their borders.

On the other hand, countries like Norway that perceive the threat to be strongly indirect (that is, they concede the threat

Table 4: General Comparison of Country Characteristics

Country	Relative Importance of Maritime Interests to Economy	Merchant Navy Size	Offshore Petroleum	Perception Of Threat	Immigration - Percentage Non-Western - Control	State Isolation Or Independence	National Security Legislation	Priority Of Key Activities	Best Practices	Proactive Or Reactive
Australia	High	Small	Small	Direct	~20% - Via Sea - Tight control	High	Aggressive	C,DA,S,R	2C, 2DA	Proactive
Netherlands	High	Large	Medium	Indirect To Direct	~10% - Via Land - Open – changing to tight	Low	Aggressive (Recent)	C,S,R,DA	1C, 1S	Proactive
Norway	High	Large	Large	Indirect	~5% - Via Air - Tight control	High	Traditional	R,DA,S,C	1R	Reactive
Canada	Medium	Small	Medium	Indirect	~17% - Via Air - Open	Medium	Aggressive	C,DA,S,R	---	Reactive

exists but believe it to be directed towards other countries) are more inclined to weigh reactive activities the highest so they preserve their independence of policy selection and provide insurance for what they already possess. The Netherlands, a deeply multicultural country which has a growing unease about the internal threat and one which is permanently linked to the complex and interwoven EU, needs collaboration to survive in the regional community but ranks safeguarding very high due to its importance as a major maritime trading hub for that same community.

Therefore, based on their perceptions of the threat, the three case-countries vary proportionally in the level of priority given to preventive activities, and inversely in the level of priority given to reactive response. If one desired to increase the preventive nature of national response, the perception of direct threat on that state's interests and values would have to increase.

Several other broad conclusions present themselves from the analysis of the case-countries and their best practices. In all instances there was friction between legislation for national security and legislation for civil liberties. To enable government agencies to collect information and allow the sharing of information and intelligence both vertically and horizontally, laws have been enacted which may compromise hard-fought civil liberty laws. The ability to share information between federal departments and local responders to close the seams that terrorists utilize inevitably comes at the price of some individual privacy for citizens. Countries that perceive a direct threat to their security are more likely to allow compromise to their state's civil liberties than ones that do not. This relationship is exacerbated when a state's immigrant population is seen to pose an internal threat.

The size of a state's merchant marine has very little to do with the selection of priorities for maritime security, at least from this sample of cases. The fact that merchant ships can spend most of their existence away from the flag country's ports decreases the importance of their security with respect to homeland maritime security. However, a merchant marine is likely to increase a country's desire to promote global maritime security. On the other hand, fixed maritime interests such as offshore platforms (which sometimes are crucial to a state's economic well-being) tend to increase the importance of reactive activities in order to protect a known asset on home soil (or seabed).

A particular conclusion can be made for maritime domain awareness outside of territorial waters. As the experience of the Netherlands will attest, at a certain point, the complexity of vessel traffic passing by one's coasts becomes overwhelming thus decreasing the importance as one travels away from the coast. Complexity stemming from multiple partners in vessel traffic management as well as extremely dense traffic, makes domain awareness less attractive to invest in than other security activities which then take priority. The traffic has such high volume and is so confusing in the channel that the Netherlands has chosen to leave tracking and awareness to the ships themselves and other states outside of Dutch territorial waters. In their risk management solution, the Dutch feel that they can live with the uncertainty outside their territorial waters—instead, they beef up safeguarding and response so that if a problem occurs, they can react.

Finally, it is apparent from the case analysis that countries which are independent of regional partners or dominant in a particular region have more flexibility in selecting the nature of their security laws and their national responses to the perceived threat. The compromises that stem from interaction and interdependence often help to set the tone for a state's security policy development and law-making.

These general conclusions are of interest to governments which seek to strike a correct balance for their legislation and policy in maritime security. While each country has a different strategic nexus, these general findings could be helpful in policy discussion during the development of national and maritime security policies. A common trend in all countries is the addition of security-based scrutiny of policy—i.e., scrutiny to determine the security implications of a policy—including economic, social, political and environmental policy. One of the legacies of 9/11 is thus the recognition that the pillar of security is inter-related with the other pillars of a democratic state, and cannot be downplayed in the age of strategic terrorism.

As for Canada, the Standing Senate Committee on National Security and Defence has documented the strengths and weaknesses of the Canadian maritime security system and has made sweeping recommendations with regard to how this system should be improved by government.[1] A substantial amount of progress has been made. Yet, the vast majority of Canadians still perceive the threat to Canada to be indirect. Thus, the various proactive approaches that are being initiated by the government are often underfunded, lack strategic coherency and display conflicted leadership.

If a more preventive approach is indeed required in Canada's situation, the widespread education of Canadians, and more importantly, Canadian politicians, about strategic terrorism and its relationship to Canada and Canadian maritime interests is an important process in which the government should engage. Canadians have to appreciate the level of the threat to Canada and what forms the terrorist threat takes in Canada. Moreover, they must understand that Canada can also be a conduit for threats to the United States, and that being the means through which the United States is attacked would threaten Canada in terms of damaged relations with our most important trade partner. Government organizations that deal with information concerning activities of terrorists in Canada will have to declare their successes and defeats when national security will allow it. Canadians have to know that the terrorist battlespace exists in Canada. To adopt a culture of prevention, in any form, Canadians must feel the need—they must perceive a direct threat.

Furthermore, the healthy friction that exists between civil

rights and national security must be understood by Canadians. Like the countries studied in here, Canada must engage more fully in the debate over the need to challenge existing legislation and interpretation of policy in the light of the changed battlespace. The passing of the anti-terrorism bill and the *Public Safety Act* demonstrate that this debate has commenced. However, many issues (such as information-sharing and interoperability across government, privacy and *Charter of Rights* concerns, etc) have not been pursued with vigour. To achieve a proactive stance (which would accompany a direct perception), Canada needs to engage more fully.

The content of the laws relating to security also proves that Canada, like many other countries which are struggling to resolve these issues, is approaching the matter in a piecemeal fashion which treats individual problems in a one-off manner. There has not yet been a strategic-level debate on the issue that covers the full range of community concerns that national security raises and those concerns that individual and privacy rights raise. While there are a number of ongoing commissions and enquiries, there is no government-led, coordinated debate on issues like information-sharing and interoperability which are the foundations of an integrated government mechanism espoused by the national security policy. The preventive, "integrated" approach to national and maritime security that is envisioned in the new National Security Policy (NSP) will not be optimized unless such a debate occurs. Collaboration, information-sharing and proactive measures will be limited in Canada unless the fundamental debate over civil rights and national security is undertaken in a focused and coordinated fashion and legislation is enacted to convey the results of the debate.

Finally, now that Canada has a fledgling national security policy, the time is right for a maritime security strategy which takes lessons from the case studies in this paper and blends ocean governance into the strategic mix that the NSP presents. In the maritime security strategy, economic, social, security, environmental and political issues should be considered in ocean governance. By using the four key government activities—collaboration, domain awareness, safeguarding and responsiveness—the maritime environment can be strategically organized to include international concerns, coastal concerns (especially the Arctic *now*), internal waterways (including dams and canals), maritime infrastructure (including oil rigs), and the governance to manage it all.

As this effort continues over the next decade (for that is how long change of this nature will take), the conclusions from this paper could be helpful in finding the optimum solutions for the Canadian context of maritime security. In particular, the seven best practices that have been extracted from the three case-countries, that have much in common with Canada but offer a wide scope of strategic variance, will provide strong policy options for a government that is destined to experience ongoing debates about improved maritime and national security.

Notes

1.   Senate of Canada, "Canada's Coastlines: The Longest Under-Defended Borders in the World," pp. 147-160.

BIBLIOGRAPHY

Akerboom, Eric. "Counter-terrorism in the Netherlands." Available from the Federation of American Scientists website, at http://www.fas.org/irp/world/ netherlands/ct.pdf (Cited 15 September 2004).

Australia. Defence White Paper. *Defence 2000: Our Future Defence Force*. Canberra: Department of Defence, 2000. Available from http://www.defence.gov.au/whitepaper/ (Cited 15 September 2004).

Australia. Parliamentary Joint Committee on the National Crime Authority. Hearings on National Crime Authority, Mr. Raymond Kendall, Secretary General of Interpol. Canberra: NCA 8, 1996. Available from http://www.aph.gov.au/ hansard/joint/commttee/j5963242.pdf (Cited 15 September 2004).

Australia. Parliamentary Joint Committee on the National Crime Authority. *Annual Report 1996-1997*. Canberra, 1997. Available from http://www.aph.gov.au/ Senate/committee/acc_ctte/annual/1996/report2/contents.htm (Cited September 2004).

Australia. Prime Minister's Office. "Commonwealth and States and Territories Agreement on Terrorism and Multi-jurisdictional Crime." Canberra, April 2002. Available from http://www.nationalsecurity.gov.au/agd/www/rwpattach.nsf/viewasattachmentpersonal/(2A296B295C1E058B328FED2164E40B7D)~IGA+as+at+22+October.doc/$file/IGA+as+at+22+October.doc (Cited 15 September 2004).

Australia. "The Australian Secret Intelligence Service (ASIS) Information." Canberra: March 2004. Available from http://www.asis.gov.au/about.html (Cited 15 September 2004).

Avis, Peter. "Surveillance and Canadian Maritime Domestic Security." In *Canadian Military Journal*, Vol 4, No. 1 (Spring 2003), pp. 9-14.

Ayson, Robert. "Australia's Defence and Security Challenges: A Tale of Three 'Posts.'" In *New Zealand International Review* (January/February 2003), pp. 10-14.

Barber, Benjamin. *Jihad vs. McWorld*. New York: Ballantine Books, 2001.

Barry, Micheal, Ina Elema and Paul van der Molen. "Ocean Governance in the Netherlands North Sea." In *FIG (Federation Internationales des Geometres) Working Week 2003*. Paris, 2003. Available from http://www.fig.net/pub/fig_2003/TS_20/ TS20_2_Barry_et_al.pdf (Cited 15 September 2004).

Bercuson, D.J. "Canada-US Defence Relations Post-11 September." In David Carment, Fen Osler Hampson and Norman Hillmer (eds). *Canada Among Nations 2003: Coping with the American Colossus*. Toronto: Oxford University Press, 2003, pp. 121-134.

Berkowitz, Bruce. "Intelligence and the War on Terrorism." In *Orbis: A Journal of World Affairs*, Vol. 46, No. 2 (Spring 2002), pp. 289-300.

—. "Spying in the Post-September 11 World," in *Hoover Digest*, Vol. 20 (Fall 2003), pp. 1-8. Available from http://www-hoover.stanford.edu/publications/digest/034/berkowitz.html (Cited 15 September, 2004).

Bland, Douglas. "Canada's Mechanism for the Higher Direction of Defence Security: The Next Generation," Conference Paper, Institute for Research on Public Policy, November 2000. Available from http://www.irpp.org/books/index.htm (Cited 15 September 2004).

Boulden, Jane. "A National Security Council for Canada?" Claxton Papers No. 2, School of Policy Studies, Queen's University, Kingston, 2000.

Brailey, Malcolm. "Australia's Approach to 'Homeland Security.'" In *Institute of Defense and Strategic Studies (IDSS) Commentaries* (August 2003), 2. Available from http://www.ntu.edu.sg/idss/Perspective/research_050330.htm (Cited 15 September 2004).

Brown, S.A. *Breakthrough Customer Service: Best Practices of Leaders in Customer Support*. Toronto: John Wiley and Sons, 1997.

Canada. "Canadian Security and Military Preparedness: The Government's Response to the Report of the Standing Senate Committee on National Security and Defence." Ottawa: Queen's Printers,

October 2002.

Canada. "Government of Canada Announces up to $172.5 Million in New Marine Security Projects," Government of Canada News Release No. GC001/03, 22 January 2003. Available from http://www.tc.gc.ca/mediaroom/releases/nat/ 2003/03-gc001.htm (Cited 15 September 2004).

Canada. Department of National Defence. *Strategic Assessment 2002*. Ottawa: Directorate of Strategic Analysis Policy Planning Division, 2002.

Canada. Department of National Defence. *White Paper on Defence Policy*. Ottawa: Government of Canada, 1994.

Canada. Department of Transport. *Enhancing the Security of Canada's Marine Transportation System*. Ottawa: Interdepartmental Marine Security Working Group, 2004.

Canada. Department of Transport. *The Canadian Marine Act – Beyond Tomorrow: Report of the Review Panel to the Minister of Transport*. Ottawa: Queen's Printers, 2003.

Canada. House of Commons. "Facing Our Responsibilities, The State of Readiness of the Canadian Armed Forces." In *Report of the Standing Committee on National Defence and Veteran Affairs*, 37th Parliament, 2nd Session, May 2002.

Canada. Privy Council Office. *Securing an Open Society: Canada's National Security Policy*. Ottawa: Government of Canada, April 2004.

Canada. Privy Council Office. *The Canadian Security and Intelligence Community: Helping Keep Canada and Canadians Safe and Secure*. Ottawa: Queen's Printers, 2000.

Canada. Senate. *The Report of the Special Senate Committee of Security and Intelligence*, 36th Parliament, 1st Session, January 1999.

Canada. Senate. "Canada's Coastlines: The Longest Under-Defended Borders in the World." In *Report of the Standing Senate Committee on National Security and Defence*, 37th Parliament, 2nd Session, Vol. I, October 2003.

Canada. Senate. "Canada's Coastlines: The Longest Under-Defended Borders in the World." In *Report of the Standing Senate Committee on National Security and Defence*, 37th Parliament, 2nd Session, Vol. II, October 2003.

Canada. Senate. "Canadian Security and Military Preparedness." In *Report of the Standing Senate Committee on National Security and Defence*, 37ᵗʰ Parliament, 2ⁿᵈ Session, February 2002.

Canada. Senate. "National Emergencies: Canada's Fragile Frontlines." In *Report of the Standing Senate Committee on National Security and Defence*, 37ᵗʰ Parliament, 2ⁿᵈ Session, Vol. I, March 2004.

Crickard, Fred W. and Haydon, Peter T. *Why Canada Needs Maritime Forces*. Halifax: The Naval Officers' Association of Canada, Napier Publishing Inc., 1994.

Coulter, Daniel, "Globalization of Maritime Commerce: The Rise of Hub Ports." In Sam J. Tangredi (ed.). *Globalization and Maritime Power*. Washington: National Defense University, 2002. Available from http://www.ndu.edu/inss/ books/Books_2002/ Globalization_and_ Maritime_Power_Dec_02/08_ch07.htm (Cited 15 September 2004), pp. 133-142.

Delvoie, Louis A. "Canada and International Security Operations: The Search for Policy Rationales." *Canadian Military Journal*, Vol. 1, No. 2 (Summer 2000), pp. 13-24.

—. "Curious Ambiguities: Reflections on Canada's International Security Policy." Conference Paper, Institute for Research on Public Policy, November 2000. Available from http://www.irpp.org/ indexe.htm (Cited 15 September 2004).

DeMille, Dianne. "Australia's Coastwatch – What Can Canada Learn?" *Canadian American Strategic Review* (July 2003). Available from http://www.sfu.ca/casr/ft-ozcusdd1.htm (Cited 15 September 2004).

Elcock, Ward, Director, Canadian Security Intelligence Service. "The John Tait Memorial Lecture." Presentation given 17 October 2003 at the CASIS Conference in Vancouver, BC, Canada. Available from http://www.csis-scrs.gc.ca/eng/miscdocs/ director20031017 _e.html (Cited 17 September 2004).

European Union. "Council Framework Decision of 13 June 2002 on the European Arrest Warrant and the Surrender Procedures between Member States." In *Official Journal of the European Communities*. Brussels: European Union Press, July 2002.

Grabo, Cynthia. *Anticipating Surprise: Analysis for Strategic Warning*. Washington: The Joint Military Intelligence College, December 2002.

Haydon, Peter. "Sea Power and Maritime Strategy in the 21st Century: A "Medium" Power Perspective." *Maritime Security Occasional Paper No. 10*. Halifax: Centre for Foreign Policy Studies, 2000.

Herman, Micheal. *Intelligence Power in Peace and War*. Cambridge: Cambridge University Press, 1996.

Hersch, Seymour. "The Stovepipe." *The New Yorker*, 27 October 2003, pp. 77-89.

Holmes, John. *Life with Uncle: The Canadian-American Relationship*. Toronto: University of Toronto Press, 1981.

Howard, John. "Strategic Leadership for Australia: Policy Directions in a Complex World." Lecture delivered by Prime Minister Howard at the meeting of the Committee for Economic Development Australia, 20 November 2002.

Keehley, Patricia, et al. *Benchmarking for Best Practices in the Public Sector: Achieving Performance Breakthroughs in Federal, State, and Local Agencies*. San Francisco: Jossey-Bass Publishers, 1997.

Krohn Devold, Kristen. Norwegian Minister of Defence. "The Norwegian Defence – Usability through Transformation." Speech delivered by Defence Minister Krohn Devold at the meeting of the Norwegian Atlantic Committee, Oslo, 2 February 2004. Available from http://www.atlanterhavskomiteen.no/ publikasjoner/andre/i-tekster/20.htm (Cited 16 September 2004).

Leopold, Reuven. "The Next Naval Revolution." In *Jane's Navy International* (January/February 1996), pp. 8-20.

Macnamara, W.D. and Ann Fitz-Gerald. "A National Security Framework for Canada." *Institute for Research on Public Policy: Policy Matters*, Vol. 3, No. 10 (October 2002), pp. 1-28.

Martin, Paul. *Making History: The Politics of Achievement*. Ottawa: paulmartin Inc., 2003.

Mason, Dwight. "US-Canada Defence Relations." In David Carment, Fen Osler Hampson and Norman Hillmer (eds). *Canada Among Nations 2003: Coping with the American Colossus*. Toronto: Oxford University Press, 2003, pp. 135-155.

Navy League of Canada. "Canada, An Incomplete Maritime Nation." In *Maritime Affairs*. Ottawa: The Navy League of Canada, 2003. Available from http://www.navyleague.ca/eng/ma/2003paper.asp

(Cited 15 September 2004).

Netherlands. Ministry of Defence. *Defence White Paper 2000*. Netherlands, Ministry of Defence, 1999.

Netherlands. Parliament. *The Intelligence and Security Services Act 2002*. The Hague: Government Press, 2002. Available from www.fas.org/irp/world/netherlands/ intel-act-2002.doc (Cited 15 September 2004).

Norway. Ministry of Defence. *Norwegian Defence 2004*. Ministry of Defence website, 2004. Available from http://odin.dep.no/fd/ engelsk/publ/veiledninger/010011-120064/index-dok000-b-n-a.html (Cited 15 September 2004).

Norway. Ministry of Defence. *The Norwegian Defence Budget 2004*. Norwegian Department of Defence website (8 October 2003). Available from http://odin.dep.no/fd/engelsk/ aktuelt/pressem/ 010001-070028/dok-bn.html (Cited 16 September 2004).

O'Brien, Kevin and Erik van de Linde, et al. "Quick Scan of post 9/11 National Counter-terrorism Policymaking and Implementation in Selected European Countries." *Counter-terrorism in Europe*. RAND Organization website. Available from http://www.rand.org/ randeurope/review/1.4-obrien.html (Cited 15 September 2004).

"Overview of Customs Coastwatch." In *The Australian Journal of Emergency Management*, Vol. 18, No. 3 (August 2003), pp. 1-8.

Pratt, David. "Foreign Intelligence in the New Security Environment." In David Rudd and David McDonough (eds). *Canadian Strategic Forecast 2004 – The 'New Security Environment': Is the Canadian Military up to the Challenge?* Toronto: The Canadian Institute of Strategic Studies, 2004, pp. 3-10.

Riste, Olav. "'The Missing Dimension': The Diplomatic History of Intelligence." In Jenssen and Riste (eds). *Intelligence in the Cold War*. Oslo: NIDS, 2001, pp. 135-147.

Rudner, Martin. "Contemporary Threats, Future Tasks: Canadian Intelligence and the Challenges of Global Security." In N. Hillmer and M.A. Molot (eds). *Canada Among Nations 2002: A Fading Power*. Don Mills, Ontario: Oxford University Press, 2002, pp. 141-171.

—. "Hunters and Gatherers: The Intelligence Coalition Against Islamic Terrorism." In *International Journal of Intelligence and*

CounterIntelligence, Vol. 17, No. 2 (Summer 2004), pp. 193-230.

—. "Challenge and Response: Canada's Intelligence Community and the War on Terrorism." In *Canadian Foreign Policy*, Vol. 11, No. 2 (Winter 2004), pp. 17-40.

Stern, Jessica. "The Protean Enemy." In *Foreign Affairs*, Vol. 82, No. 4 (July/August 2003), pp. 21-39.

Stevenson, Jonathan. "How Europe and America Defend Themselves." In *Foreign Affairs*, Vol. 82, No. 2 (March/April 2003), pp. 78-89.

Tewes, A., L. Rayner and K. Kavanaugh. *A Foundation Paper on Australia's Maritime Strategy*. A research paper prepared at client request and made available to the Joint Standing Committee on Foreign Affairs, Defence and Trade. Canberra: Australian Government Publishing Service, 2002.

Treverton, Gregory. "Balancing Security and Liberty in the War on Terror." Presentation given at Information Sharing and Homeland Security Conference, Syracuse University Faculty of Law, New York, 19 March 2004. Available from http://www.maxwell.syr.edu/campbell/Library%20Papers/Event%20papers/ISHS/Treverton.pdf (Cited 15 September 2004).

United States. *The National Security Strategy of the United States of America*. Washington, DC: US Government Printing Office, 2003.

United States. Central Intelligence Agency. *The World Factbook 2004*. Washington, DC Database online. Available from http://www.cia.gov/cia/publications/factbook/index.html (Cited 15 September 2004).

Van Buuren, Jelle. "Country Report – Netherlands," The Association for Progressive Communications website (2001). Available from http://europe.rights.apc.org/ c_rpt/netherlands.html (Cited 16 September 2004).